Perspectives
on the
Middle School

M. Ann Grooms
The University of Cincinnati

and

Innovation-Dissemination Division
Institute for Development
of Educational Activities

Charles E. Merrill Publishing Company Columbus, Ohio
A Bell & Howell Company

373. 236
G 875p

Library of Congress Catalog Number: 67-21866

Standard Book Number:
675-09733-9 (hardbound edition)
675-09732-0 (paperbound edition)

2 3 4 5 6 7 8 9 10 11 12 13 14 15-76 75 74 73 72 71 70 69 68

preface

Many studies and investigations in the education of 10-to 14-year-old children indicates that new school programs are needed for this age group. *Perspectives on the Middle School* provides insight into the implementation of a middle school program and offers a new and different educational plan.

Perspectives on the Middle School emphasizes the importance of placing learning responsibility upon the student and the role of the teacher as a guide and counselor in the learning situation. Resources have not been previously available to implement fully the student's learning responsibility. Educational technology, learning theory, and learning strategies, however, are now being sufficiently developed to enable the introduction of educational innovations into the middle school program, thereby making the placing of learning responsibility possible.

The book is suitable for use in both undergraduate and graduate education courses; in addition, it can be considered a reference book for in-service professionals. It is intended not only to serve as a useful guide for school systems and communities engaged in middle school planning, but also to supply a departure in thinking for the numerous workshops and conferences that are held to plan for middle schools. Since a broad spectrum of reader interest and background is anticipated, highly technical data is avoided, yet an effort is made to provide sufficient detail about staff, program, and plant to stimulate the professional educator. The first two chapters are directed primarily toward persons who have only limited background concerning the middle school. The last chapter should intrigue the student readers and give the professionals cause to re-evaluate their educational forecast for the post-1975 period.

iii

The writer is indebted to numerous persons for help-ful suggestions, encouragement, and advice in the scop-ing and structuring of the book. Among those persons to whom the author is especially obligated are Dr. Margaret Mead, Dr. Stuart E. Dean, Dr. Robert L. Walter, and Dr. William L. Carter.

table of contents

photo credits

FRONTISPIECE

Del Mar Intermediate School, Del Mar, California. Photo by Rondal Partridge, Berkeley, California.

CHAPTER 1

Del Mar Intermediate School, Del Mar, California. Photo by Rondal Partridge, Berkeley, California.

CHAPTER 2

New Lincoln School. Photo by Hella Hammid. Courtesy of Educational Facilities Laboratories, Inc., New York.

CHAPTER 4

UNIFIED ARTS: Amory Middle School, Amory, Mississippi. Photo by Frank Lotz Miller, New Orleans, Louisiana. Courtesy of Educational Facilities Laboratories, Inc., New York.

INDEPENDENT STUDY: Fox Lane Middle School, Mt. Kisco, New York, Photo by Phokion Karas, Melrose, Mass. Courtesy of Educational Facilities Laboratories, Inc., New York.

LANGUAGE LABORATORY: Del Mar Intermediate School, Del Mar, California, Photo by Rondal Partridge, Berkeley, California.

CHAPTER 5

Spacious School Site—Mattlin School, Courtesy of Educational Facilities Laboratories, Inc., New York.

STUDENT CENTER: Barrington Middle School, Barrington Illinois. Photo by Tony Kelly. Courtesy of Educational Facilities Laboratories, Inc., New York.

CARREL-RETRIEVAL OF INFORMATION: Photo by Eliot W. Todd, Woodbridge, Connecticut. Courtesy of Educational Facilities Laboratories, Inc., New York.

STUDY CARREL: Fox Lane Middle Schools, Mt. Kisco, New York. Courtesy of Educational Facilities Laboratories, Inc., New York.

PLANETARIUM: Barrington Middle School, Barrington, Illinois. Photo by Tony Kelly. Courtesy of Educational Facilities, Inc., New York.

LIBRARY-MATERIALS CENTER: The Perkins and Will Partnership. Chicago, Illinois. Courtesy of Educational Facilities Laboratories, Inc., New York.

FOX LANE COMMON FACILITY: Mt. Kisco, New York. Courtesy of Educational Facilities Laboratories, Inc., New York.

The School
and the
Students

Introduction

The Fox Lane Middle School is dedicated, "To each pupil who enters—that each may discover his own talents for learning and for growth." The school is housed in a beautiful new plant located in Mount Kisco, New York. Students will be educated there during their middle school years.

The Fox Lane dedication is appropriate for the numerous middle schools that have come into being since the 1950's. Middle schools are developing to meet the requirements for more effective education for older children and preadolescents. That more effective education is needed is corroborated in the views presented here by an eminent American anthropologist, Margaret Mead. Dr. Mead notes that it is a tragedy that millions of students exist who are "Condemned by social circumstances to learn very little at school and to live a life in which their potentialities are practically unrealized" (17).

Existing conditions in the junior high school may be contributing to this situation. Dr. Mead notes that the junior high school was begun without regard for known facts concerning differences between boys and girls in their preteen and early adolescent years. As a result of this oversight and of an escalating student precocity rate in recent years, we have in the 1960's an institution that is failing to meet its intellectual obligations to its students. Dr. Mead sees the junior high school as emphasizing social rather than intellectual preparation (18). She credits current educational practices with creating unfavorable student reaction to schools. The anthropologist was quoted as saying in an interview in 1961, "We have made school incredibly boring and wasteful so that bright and stupid students alike want to get through with it and out into the world" (18).

The seeds were sown for inadequate education for older children and early adolescents during the formative period of the junior high school movement. The early advocates may have mistaken the causes for the school drop-out problem of their time. It was alleged that since two-thirds of the pupils dropped out of school by the ninth grade, the predominant school organization pattern, an 8-4 arrangement, was a major contributing withdrawal factor. Educators believed that the holding power of the school could be increased by introducing secondary school experiences into grades seven and eight. As time subsequently proved, the real causes for school drop-out lay in the socio-economic realm. By 1930, three-fourths of the school's pupils continued in the 9th grade (7). The fundamental premise upon which the movement was based is passe, but junior high school supporters continue to find other reasons for retaining some type of junior high school system (6). The institution has advocates with vested interests who strongly resist attempts to change any facet of the structure or program.

Alexander and Williams state that the junior high school is most often defended on the grounds of its bridge function (1). The bridge function, which supposedly serves to

facilitate transition from elementary to high school, ought
to be discernible in the adaptation that entering high school
students make to that institution. If the high school drop-out
problem is a fair indication of how well the bridge is operating, it is time to scrutinize the bridge idea. Rather than
easing the transition problem, the junior high school may
well be alienating the student toward educational achievement later. Educational leaders have discerned an alarming
difference in student attitudes toward their personal responsibility for learning during the past 20 years. Dr. Golding,
the President of Wright State University, recently voiced a
concern for the attitudes of students enrolled at the university. The students, he contends, come to the university to be
taught, not to acquire learning through their own diligent
study efforts. As social scientists and persons from the medical
profession have become more knowledgeable about the
social, physical, and intellectual aspects of older children
and preadolescents, the purposes and practices of the junior
high school are being sharply criticized.

Berman states that "in the midst of deciding who they
are, they shouldn't have to waste any energy finding out
where they are—during the highly volatile years of 11 (sic)
through 13 or 14, youngsters should have a familiar, secure
background in which to operate" (2). Hull seems to indicate
that the familiar, secure background is not available in the
junior high school (15). "The complex junior high school
with its huge enrollment, its frequent class changes, its
teachers meeting 150 students a day, and its students being
jostled about among all these strangers every 40 minutes all
day long is too often a six or seven-ring circus instead of an
educational institution." Margaret Mead's reaction to the
junior high schools relative to the dullness of program is
corroborated by the 8th grade shadow studies of Lounsbury
and Marani. The investigators concluded that the learning
environment "was often unstimulating. There was a lack of
diversity in the program of required subjects; and there was
little provision for individual differences among pupils"(16).

A study by Dacus of pupils in grades 5 through 10 purports to show that on the measures of social, emotional, and physical maturity, and opposite sex choices, the least differences were discerned between students in grades 6 and 7 (10). If the junior high school is as Hull states, ". . . one of America's blunders that was gone into for reasons that were not educationally sound," American educators have an obligation to consider the formulation of alternate means for educating students during their middle years (15).

The identification of deficiencies in existing practices leads to new approaches toward late childhood and preadolescent schooling. The educational programs for middle schoolers are being planned to provide educational opportunities in accord with the Fox Lane dedication theme. We choose to call the type of education provided *middle school* education.

Dr. Carter V. Good's *Dictionary of Education* describes the middle school as "the school administrative unit on the secondary level containing the grades that follow the elementary and precede the last unit in the school system. The term is usually applied to the middle unit of the 14 grade program such as the 6-4-4 plan" (12). The writer's own interpretation, arising from investigation and experience, identifies the middle school as the administrative unit following the elementary and preceding the secondary school. The middle school is a system of education developed for the 10 to 14-year-old age group. Emphasis is directed primarily neither toward the acquisition of basic skills as in the elementary school nor toward the ultimate specialization of the high school. Rather, its emphasis is upon support of the student in the learning situation as he ascertains his capabilities for learning and for orientation to his environment in light of his developing physical, social, intellectual, and psychological attributes.

The middle school student has distinguishing characteristics from his childhood and adolescent compatriots. The students in the 10-14 age group are described in the literature as being:

Vigorous, inquisitive individuals on the threshold of adulthood

Sometimes awkward and uncertain, sometimes facile and adept, often troubled by self-assessment

Frequently astonished by newly evolving powers

Assiduously requiring proper occasions for exploration and venture

Now and then capable of adult behavior and responses

Often in need of opportunities for trial and error in situations where mistakes are admittable.

The middle school system of education encompasses students, professional and nonprofessional staffs, materials, facilities, and financial resources. The school features a rational approach to the learning situation using all available resources to facilitate student learning.

Learning responsibility is shifted to the student during his middle school years. The student becomes ever more responsible for his self-development. Learning in the middle school is not a continuation of the learning skills as they have been developed in the beginning school years. The middle school student is now ready to use the skills and some of the information he has been acquiring to adapt himself to the environment in which he lives and to understand the how, what, where, when, and why of his world. The middle schooler is a practitioner. As a practitioner, he wants to fill in the voids of his notions about both the physical and abstract world. He stands ready to devote himself to inquiry in areas where he recognizes a potential payoff. He rejects attempts to undertake either physical or intellectual activities solely to please someone else. As a practitioner, he wants to make or share in decision-making processes. He wants to be responsible for the actions that he takes. The task of the middle school, then, becomes that of supporting the student with innovative learning strategies.

The leaders of the middle school movement and formulators of the principles are few. Perhaps the leading figure in the group is Dr. Charles O. Richter, Superintendent of

Schools, West Hartford, Connecticut, who had the foresight to gather a distinguished group of 17 persons representing 15 distinct disciplines to plan for the establishment of the Fox Lane School (21). Other leaders include Dr. William Alexander and Dr. Emmit Williams, Director of the Middle School Institute, University of Florida; Mr. Thomas Sobol, Director of Curriculum, Bedford Public Schools, Mount Kisco, New York; Dr. Arthur Eve, Director of Curriculum, Centerville, Ohio; Mr. Jack Reigle, Principal, Chippewa Middle School, Saginaw, Michigan; Dr. Paul Zdanowicz, known for the Brown-Bridgewater Middle-School Study in Bridgewater, Massachusetts; and Dr. John H. Fisher of Teachers College and Chairman of the New York State Education Commissioner's "Advisory Committee on Human Relations and Community Tensions."

Nature of the Middle School

Our envisioned school provides for the education of the 10 to 14-year-old student. The middle school as defined in this book reveals that organizationally the formal grade structure is deleted. The basic organizational component is the team consisting of student and teacher units. There are no formal classes in the sense that one attends mathematics for grade 7 at 0900 every day. There is no school curriculum, but there are curricula. The building(s) envisioned to house the school has separate quarters for teams and common activities. It is readily adapted to the requirements of its student body and staff.

The middle school places the emphasis upon the individual learner, the learner whose chronological age lies generally within the 10-14 age interval. The group differs from the older children in that middle schoolers are not ready to take part in extra-curricular activities associated with American high schools. The middle school affords the group an opportunity to grow up in a learning environment conducive to natural educational development.

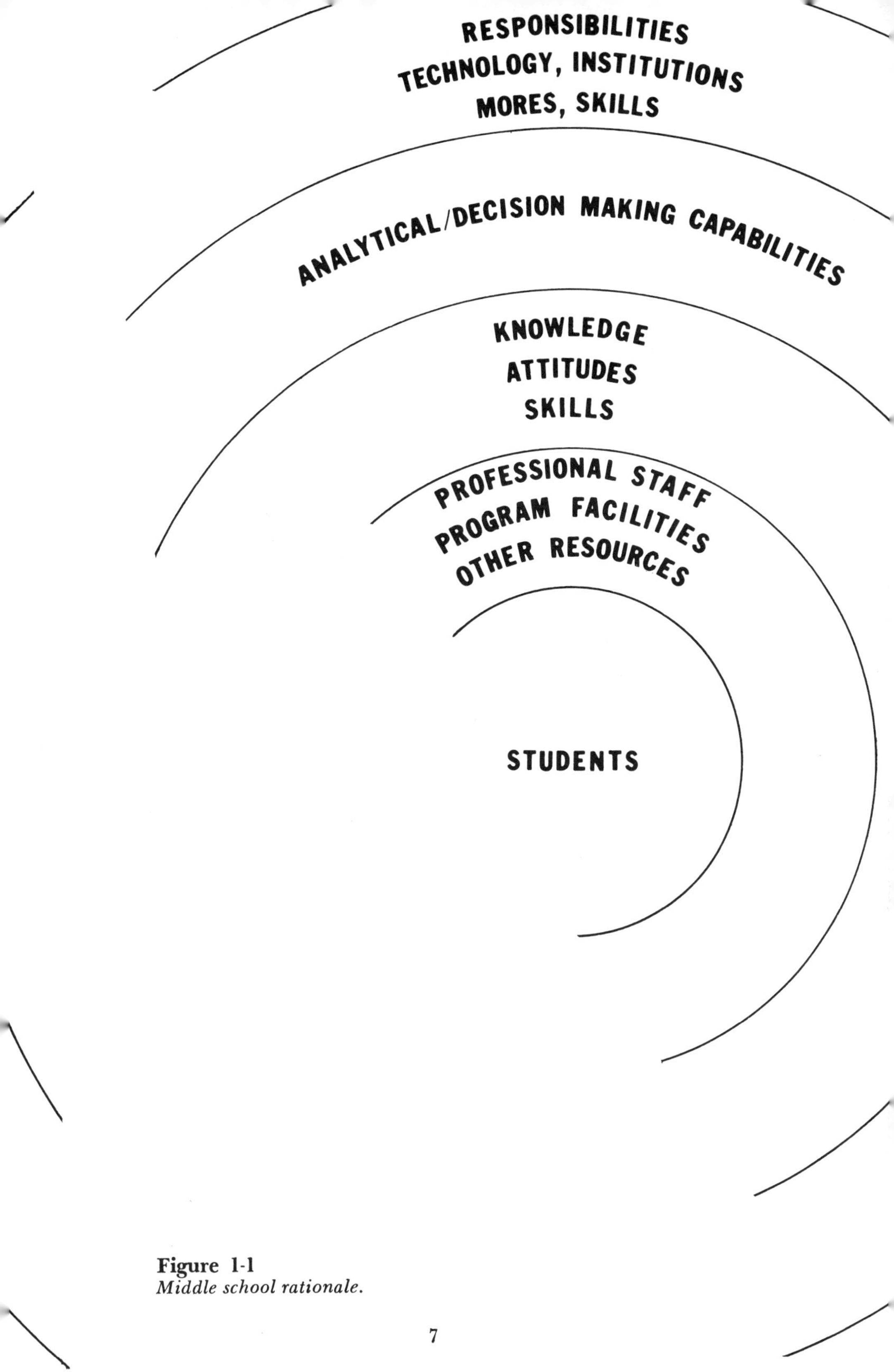

RESPONSIBILITIES
TECHNOLOGY, INSTITUTIONS
MORES, SKILLS

ANALYTICAL/DECISION MAKING CAPABILITIES

KNOWLEDGE
ATTITUDES
SKILLS

PROFESSIONAL STAFF
PROGRAM FACILITIES
OTHER RESOURCES

STUDENTS

Figure 1-1
Middle school rationale.

Middle school programs directed toward the individual
student are tailored to fit a period in the student's life when
change is rapid. The student develops from the period of
total reliance upon the parents for psychic support to a situation where an adult, external to the home, can furnish much
assurance. The changed personal need of the student dove-
tails uniquely into the student-counselor relationship pecu-
liar to middle school. The student's need to discover his own
capabilities, to understand better who he is, finds expression
in opportunities to pursue independent study, to participate
in group endeavors, and to fulfill creative desire in the fine
and practical arts. The middle school affords more effective
transition to the high school with its specialized curriculum
and often more impersonal organizational structure.

A Changing School Takes Roots

One of the middle schools opened in Bay City, Michigan,
in 1950. Its beginnings were modest. The Bay City middle
school program enrolled students in grades 5 through 8 in
self-contained classrooms. Special subjects like art, music,
homemaking and industrial arts were departmentalized. The
middle school movement has spread across the country
since that time. Institutions identified as middle schools can
be found in California, Illinois, Mississippi, Florida, Ohio
and New York, among other states.

The middle school movement is not confined to small
school systems. The nation's largest school system, New York
City, plans to establish middle schools by 1972 or 1973 (23).
Pittsburgh, Pennsylvania, will convert to middle schools over
a ten-year time period. New Haven, Connecticut, opened its
first middle schools in 1966. Other large cities are looking at
the concept to determine how it can be adapted to their
situations.

An encouraging facet of middle school growth is the
amount of time school districts spend in planning before
moving full force toward school establishment. School sys-

tems at Bridgewater, Massachusetts, Mount Kisco, New York, and Centerville, Ohio, are proceeding with middle schools only after duly considering the educational requirements for 10 to 14-year-old children. The movement needs the careful consideration devoted to it if it is to give education the maximum benefits which it inherently can supply.

Middle schools have not always started out in shining new buildings with wide-eyed and enthusiastic staffs. Quite often, the need for a new high school building results in a hand-me-down structure for the middle school. The practice of using former high school buildings can be condoned only if the structure is redesigned to meet middle school objectives. Assuming that a building with unified arts, science, and health and physical education facilities is adequate per se for a middle school program is an error. Lack of plant flexibility establishes undesirable restraints that nullify many of the educational innovations that must accompany an effective middle school program.

Many forces and factors have contributed to the growth of the middle school movement. Among these have been the recognition by leading educators that the programs in some junior high schools are inappropriate for the middle age student and that integration experiences must be provided for children during their school careers. Dr. John H. Fischer, commenting upon the recommendations for the Advisory Committee on Human Relations and Community Tensions Report to the New York State Education Commissioner that the schools of New York City be reorganized on a 4-4-4 program basis, stated: "Some junior high schools from their very earliest days became pale imitations of senior high schools. This was unfortunate because children in early adolescence do not need the kind of educational opportunities and the kinds of social and psychological programs that they need in later adolescence." Dr. Fischer explained that the 5 to 8 middle school would be feasible to furnish children with their first integration experiences. Since the new middle schools are to be fed by several neighborhood elementary schools, Fischer indicated that middle school population areas should include minority group communities. The inclusion of the minority group communities tends to result in integration of the various races in the middle school (23).

Meeting the Middle School Student

Several years ago, the author came across some songs based upon Kenya native rituals. The compositions consisted of elementary rhythms and words from the native environment. Translated, the words from one song about a vegetable went, "Pity the poor potato—he has eyes but cannot see."

Pity, too, those many educators of all levels from the kindergarten through the university who lack empathy with their students. How easy it becomes to read third hand accounts of purported studies and then to feel well versed in the latest findings relative to a particular student age group or achievement level. When exposed to the student group regarding whom the instructor considers himself to be a bona fide expert, the instructor misses the mark completely. The dearth of research conducted first-hand by professional educators has left the area by default to physicians and psychologists. Imagine, if you will then, the difficulty educators have in trying to understand the complex behavior of middle schoolers and to devise school programs that will motivate 10 to 14-year-old children.

The author has had the fortunate experience of working a number of years with middle school children. She has conducted numerous interviews, listened to the middle schoolers' problems, joined with them in success elation and has many successful student-adult friendships. Through these experiences the adult comes to know more about "out groups" and "in groups," and the values middle schoolers place upon daily events.

A number of writings prepared by middle school students, consisting of poems, short stories or extracts from short stories, have been obtained. These writings are from middle

DEL MAR INTERMEDIATE SCHOOL

schools distributed across America and reveal that regardless of where the student lives, his problems, feelings, aspirations, and attitudes are quite similar. These writings furnish background for better understanding of the middle school students.

Onc of the first and most noticeable observations about middle school students is that they are alive! A girl from Clear Cove Middle School tells us so:

> Being twelve is a life full of dreams and a heart full of hopes. It's the feeling that you belong, going downtown when everyone else does and knowing all the little secrets that everyone knows. It's acting silly when no one is around, going to the games and yelling yourself hoarse. It's getting sick from indulging too much in marshmallow sundaes, cherry cokes, and hamburgers covered with mustard and relish. It's crying over things which seem so important at the time, but which gradually disappear into the past. It's having a favorite song and telling all of those silly jokes. Yes, it's a life full of laughter, tears, and fun; but most of all it's the wonderful feeling of just being young.

Middle schoolers must be motivated to learn; otherwise, they soon slip away into daydreaming or succumb to the lure of more tempting activities (11). A girl and boy in junior high school express it this way:

Daydreams

Through my many classes here
At Van Grogh Junior High,
I very often daydream
Though I really wonder why.

My mind begins a'wandering,
Searching high and low,
For a pleasant thought or two
From the past and long ago.

I sit there very cheerfully
As though I'm in a trance,
And when French class rolls around,
I awake somewhere in France.

Daydreaming may appear to be
A lazy thing to do,
But through *your* years of schooling,
You've probably done it, too.

How I Study

Studying is a problem, agreed? But with distractions, oh boy!

To prepare myself for studying, I get a comfortable chair, some food (anything will do) , music (background, of course) , and, of all the ridiculous things, something to study. Personally, I could think of a million things more interesting to study than Teddy Roosevelt's charge up San Juan Hill, but then, I'm not the teacher.

After these preliminaries, I get comfortable, pour out some Coke, and turn the music on as loud as permissible. Finally, I hit the books. I begin to study, but I can't concentrate. How can I listen to "Surfin U.S.A." with Teddy yelling "Charge"?

By this time my fuel supply is low, so I exit and stage right to refuel. I grab anything that's handy and get back to the books. Ugh! Oh well, what can you expect from teachers? After all, they aren't preadolescents, unfortunately. Well, back to good old Teddy. Just when I get comfortable again, in troups mom with "Please turn that noise down, or else I will!"

Then I pipe up with "Mother, please! I'd rather do it myself!" So upsiedaisy to turn "Sting Ray" down to a dull roar.

After all of these distractions, I once more settle down to Teddy, but I just give up. He is too hard to concentrate on while doing the *Bossa Nova*. Then I hear the thump of size

eleven shoes and a basketball right outside. Awful, isn't it?
So I go, yelling the one word I studied, "CHARGE!"

Students' objectives are usually of a short term nature. Long
duration planning cannot be expected; tomorrow is too far
away (4). An Eden Heights middle schooler seems to agree:

Today is Alive

Today is alive,
The present is real.
It's now that is happening,
And now's what you feel.

Yesterday's dead,
It can never return.
It's over, forget it
We all live and learn.

Tomorrow's not born yet,
And no one can say
Just what will befall us
On some other day.

So live for the present
And love for today.
Today's here forever
It won't go away.

Middle school children are activity-minded; to be more
explicit, they love sports of all kinds. This piece of startling
information may surprise the reader, especially if he has
preadolescent children of his own! One "author," from Roll-
ing Meadows middle school, writes about his feelings on
sports and other matters:

Sports

I like sports,
Sports of all sorts.
I like basketball,
But I am awfully small.

I'd like to play sports night and day,
But I have school to my dismay.
But when I'm home I play and play;
So I'll take sports any old day.

When summer comes, I go away
To camp and fishing for many a day.
I do this every year, you see,
Because my mom gets sick of me.
Since I'm all muscles I'm real great, (ha)
And lousiness is what I hate.

Having whetted your curiosity to know more about this fascinating age group, it might be well to take a closer look at the middle schooler's physical and behavioral characteristics. A somewhat detailed description is set forth in the following sections.

Physical characteristics. Students in the 10 to 14 age bracket differ widely in physical attributes and maturity. Growth rates for some children is very rapid, while for others it may range from gradual to slow. The growth rate discrepancies cause some surprising effects among the students; some boys may resemble young children while some girls have the appearance of young ladies (5).

Growth rates differ between the sexes as well as within the sex group. Girls manifest rapid growth to approximately their 13th birthday after which a slow growth rate is experienced for the remainder of adolescence. They tend to be heavier and taller than boys until well into their 12th year; in fact, some attain adult height by age 14. Boys' growth rate is greater between 12 and 16 with the rate slowing after the latter age. Rapid muscular development occurs during the middle school years for both sexes (7).

Rate of maturation is influenced by race, family, climate, socio-economic status and sex. Studies show that children living in the South mature earlier than those living in the North. Negroes mature at a faster rate than caucasians. Girls tend to mature more rapidly than boys (13). Maturity differences between the sexes become obvious at the age of 11 years and reach their peak around the 14th year when female maturation may exceed that of the males by as much as two years (11).

During the latter middle school years, boys and girls develop secondary sexual characteristics, and student concern about sex and personal appearance increases. Changes in physical characteristics embarrass both sexes. Preadolescents are concerned with physical shape and size. None of them seem to be satisfied with themselves: they are too tall, too short, too fat, too thin, too underdeveloped and too clumsy (7).

Physical activities provide much satisfaction for the preadolescents. Organized team sports are enjoyed by both sexes. Students respect good sportsmanship and thrive upon competition. They are willing to submerge personal ego for team good. The individual player is highly motivated; his actions show that he has a need to prove that he can 'take" everything. The unskilled performer tends to exclude himself from play since worry about lack of skill may cause a student to be self-conscious in connection with undertaking new activities (9).

Students of the middle school are inclined toward physical overexertion. Those persons working with preadolescents must be alert to signs of overfatigue. Since the heart is not yet fully developed, hard play may result in a drop in blood pressure following fatigue. To avoid overexertion closer observance is necessary for girls' physical activities than for boys' since girls tend to tire more readily (11).

Sociological and psychological attributes. Suppose we select some books to read which deal with the effect of behavior characteristics of older children or the preadolescent. What do they say about student behavior during the middle school years? Usually the material covered emphasizes behavioral aspects which have not proven too helpful to teachers concerned with improving the effectiveness of a given topic with this age group. These books indicate that the child is afflicted with ambivalent desires during the preadolescent period, desiring freedom from his parents but fearing the loss of security. Continuing, we learn that the child forms close interrelations with his peer groups during this period, and that he may also form close associations with adults. It becomes clear that deflating and criticizing the child can have debilitating effects upon his self image (1). Such information does not represent new behavioral insights; it has long been known. Educators are not so incompetent as to fail to realize the significance of the information. However, the findings have not resulted in changed instructional practices which have greatly improved learning. The observation leads to the consideration that other factors, as yet unrecognized, may be operating that have implications for understanding actions of older children and the preadolescent.

Reflect, if you will, upon your own preadolescent days. What was your chief need? Our poetess hinted at it when she expressed joy in being young. The need is for better communications with the natural and physical world. Why does the preadolescent turn away from his parents and toward peers and other adults? Is it because of growth, chemical and organic changes in the body alone? From a purely rational viewpoint, more can be accomplished by remaining within the confines of a friendly home atmosphere than by rejecting its influence and resources. Our observation and experience with the preadolescent tells us that communication must have a substantial part to play in the situation. The middle school accepts whatever sociology and psychology has to contribute toward knowing the preadolescent and adds communications as an equally forceful factor in the student's reaction to his social world. The middle school recognizes the need for communication before any student interest can be generated in a given learning situation (20).

A number of anxieties and problems are identified by middle school students as being of concern to them. These fall into categories covering home, school, self, and peers.

Home concerns relate to family relationships, home routines such as watching TV, radio listening, and going to bed. School concerns encompass school performance, grades, and homework. Self-concern takes in sex, personality problems, losing of temper and arguing or pouting (7).

During their middle school years, students reflect different peer paragons. The author has found through her work with middle schoolers that the peer interactions shown on Figures 1-2 and 1-3 are representative of peer paragons for students in the 10 to 14 age group.

Peer acceptance is exceedingly important to future behavior patterns. Peer rejection often leads to development of solitary behavior models.

Sex may be very disturbing to middle school students. They must adjust their thinking and behavior to conform to newly experienced physiological drives and their physically changing bodies. Some girls do not want to grow up. A number of escape techniques are used in an attempt to delay the impact of maturation, including over-eating, acting like a tomboy, and being careless about their personal appearance. If the girl's relationship has been good with her parents, she will modify her close feeling toward her father and want to become like her mother. Boys also have sexual anxieties which may be shown by their staying very close to home and by being reluctant to join their peers in sports and other activities. Mother's protection may be so important to them that they would rather perform activities within the home. Home activities provide the sexually anxious boy with an opportunity to give attention to his mother and to seek her approval for actions taken (8).

Middle School Activities

The middle school recognizes the importance of providing middle schoolers with the opportunity to employ their capabilities within their real world environment. When an individual has the resources to undertake an endeavor, he looks

**Twelve
year old
student**

**Eleven
year old
student**

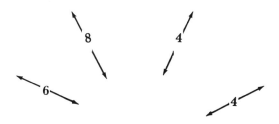

Thirteen year old student

Ten year old student

Fourteen year old student   **Ten year old student**   **Nine year old student**

Figure 1-2 *Peer paragon depicting selection of individual best
friend by a simulated group of 24 ten-year-old students.*

for a place to use them. The place for middle schoolers to try out their new learning skills, physical capabilities, and other abilities is in an activity program.

The activity program must be conceived so as to encourage the student to exploit those personal attitudes which lead to need satisfaction. This can be accomplished through participation in physical, service, aesthetic, and intellectual activities.

Physical activities. The stored-up energy and drive of 10 to 14-year-olds lead to the natural employment of physical skills in an intramural program in the middle school. Competition may be just as sharp among student teams within the school as that inspired by inter-school programs. Intramurals permit all students who desire so to participate, and it makes it feasible for student planning to conceive and outline the program. Skill development, sportsmanship and appreciation for both team and individual sports become more important than winning at any price. Student support for individual teams can prove a stimulating and effective emotional release as in any inter-school athletic program without the undesirable social side effects associated with the latter activity.

Service activities. The middle school provides many opportunities for student service. Student service activities must offer a chance to enjoy the heady experience of making decisions that affect the action of others. Students live in a world where decisions are made for them—someone else always knows what is best. Parents believe that they are serving the student's interest by making decisions that affect him, but, in truth, the student needs to serve his peers by making decisions. The student council can be a decision-making body in the middle school. When decision-making responsibility is delegated to the council, the student body can observe first-hand the importance of selecting governing officials with care. Among other duties, the student council can be delegated authority in the operation of the intramural program, orientation day, and school convocations. The obligation to fulfill the trust placed in the council by students causes council members to appreciate the importance of problems and decision-making techniques.

Student publications serve both the student body and the community by providing information. Various skills are required by the publication staff thereby affording many students the opportunity to employ their skills for the benefit of others. Student payoff comes in the esteem with which the publications are held by their readers.

Aesthetic activities. Students want to practice what they are learning. Too often, failure to employ the arts to make the school environment more pleasing results in their being considered as part of the world of unreality. The arts can be advanced by permitting the middle school aesthetically-oriented student to participate in the "live arts" such as music festivals, dramatic endeavors, arts and crafts shows, and school displays. A permissive attitude toward the arts is the catalyst needed to bring about effective arts activity.

Intellectual activities. The academic areas are the springboard for participating in intellectual activity in the middle school. Many activities in the academic area can be extended in scope and depth to afford students adequate opportunities for personal dedication. Student dedication to a purpose leads to the kinds of inquiry and investigation that are needed by middle schoolers. Intellectual activities become stimulating adventures—science, social studies, mathematics and language arts all have challenging areas. Space activities hold much interest for the middle school budding scientist. This activity lends itself to such projects as designing and fabricating equipment, studies of the space environment, and experiments in the life sciences. The social studies area presents insights that can lead to better human relations through role playing, simulation and structural situation. Mathematics becomes even more challenging to the imagination as the computer becomes more "human," and the question arises—"Can machines think?" Language arts intensify the realization that the need for increasing abilities to communicate is imperative. Interest in learning to write, organizing thoughts, and speaking can be found among students dedicated to the thesis that effective communication is a key to better success in school, home and community endeavors.

Others. Activities should involve *all* students. The new student entering a middle school will be coming into a society where activities are already in progress. He must find a place for himself in that society. The teaching team has the responsibility for making the assimilation of students into the society as effective as possible.

REFERENCES

1. Alexander, W. M. and E. L. Williams. "Schools for the Middle Years." *Educational Leadership,* 23:217-23; December, 1965.

2. Berman, Sidney. "As a Psychiatrist See Pressures on Middle Class Teenagers," *Historical Education Association Journal,* 54:17-24; February, 1965.

3. Bloom, Benjamin S. *Stability and Change in Human Characteristics.* New York: John Wiley and Sons, 1964.

4. Blos, Peter. *On Adolescence.* New York: The Free Press of Glencoe, Inc., 1962.

5. Breckenridge, Marian E. and Vincent E. Lee. *Child Development, Physical and Psychological Growth Through Adolescence.* Philadelphia: W. B. Saunders Company, 1965.

6. Cole, Luella. *Psychology of Adolescence.* New York: Holt, Rinehart and Winston, 1961.

7. Coleman, James S. *The Adolescent Society.* Glencoe, Illinois: The Free Press, 1961.

8. Conant, James Bryant. *Education in the Junior High School Years.* Princeton, New Jersey, 1960.

9. ————. *Slums and Suburbs: A Commentary on Schools in Metropolitan Areas.* New York: McGraw-Hill Book Co., Inc., 1961.

10. Dacus, W. P. *A Grade Structure For the Early Adolescent Years.* Houston: Bureau of Educational Research and Services, 1963.

11. Gesell, Arnold and Frances L. Ilg and Louise Bates Ames. *Youth the Years from Ten to Sixteen.* New York: Harper & Row, Publishers, 1965.

12. Good, Carter V. *Dictionary of Educational Research.* New York: McGraw-Hill Book Company, 1959.

13. Hollien, Harry, Ellen Malcik and Barbara Hollien. "Adolescent Voice Change in Southern White Males." *Speech Monographs,* 32:87-90; March, 1965.

14. Johnson, Eric W. *How to Live Through Junior High School.* Philadelphia: J. B. Lippincott Company, 1959.

15. Hull, J. H. "Are Junior High Schools the Answer." *Educational Leadership,* 23:213-216; December, 1965.

16. Lounsbury, John and Jean Marani. *The Junior High School We Saw: One Day in the Eighth Grade.* Washington, D. C.: Association for Supervision and Curriculum Development, 1964.

17. McClelland, David C. "Motivation Can Be Developed," *Harvard Business Review,* 6-24; December, 1965.

18. Mead, Margaret. "Are We Squeezing Out Adolescence? *The Educational Digest,* 26:3-7; November, 1960.

19. ————. "Early Adolescence in the United States." *The Bulletin of the National Association of Secondary School Principals,* 49:5-10; April, 1965.

20. ————. "We're Robbing Our Children of Childhood." *Rochester Democrat and Chronicle,* May 21, 1961.

21. Murphy, Judith. *Middle Schools.* New York: Educational Facilities Laboratories, Inc., 1965.

22. Schmuch, Richard. "Concerns of Contemporary Adolescents." *The Bulletin of the National Association of Secondary-School Principals,* 49:19-28; April, 1965.

23. Scholastic Teacher Interviews: Dr. John H. Fischer. *Scholastic Teacher,* September 23, 1964.

SELECTED READINGS

Ahmann, J. Stanley and Marvin D. Glock. *Evaluating Pupil Growth,* 2nd ed. Boston: Allyn and Bacon, Inc., 1963.

Anderson, Robert H. "The Junior High School." *Architectural Record,* 129:126-131; January, 1961.

Association for Supervision and Curriculum Development. *Freeing Capacity to Learn.* Washington, D.C.: National Education Association, 1960.

Baller, Warren R. *The Psychology of Human Growth and Development.* New York: Holt, Rinehart and Winston, Inc., 1961.

Beck, Robert H. "Society and Individuals." *Individualizing Instruction,* Sixty-first Yearbook of the National Society for the Study of Education, Part I. Chicago: University Press, 1962.

Boutwell, W. D. "What's Happening in Education? What are Middle Schools?" *PTA Magazine,* 60:14; December, 1965.

Brimm, R. P. *The Junior High School.* Washington, D.C.: The Center for Applied Research in Education, Inc., 1963.

Brown, B. Frank. *The Nongraded High School.* Englewood Cliffs, New Jersey: Prentice-Hall, Inc., 1964.

Bruner, Jerome S. "Education As Social Invention." *Saturday Review* 70-72, 102-104; February, 1966.

————. *On Knowing.* Cambridge, Massachusetts: Harvard University Press, 1962.

————. *The Process of Education.* Cambridge, Massachusetts: Harvard University Press, 1963.

Burton, William H. and Roland B. Kimball and Richard L. Wing. *Education for Effective Thinking.* New York: Appleton-Century-Crofts, Inc., 1960.

Chickering, Arthur W. "Dimensions of Independence." *Journal of Higher Education,* 35:38-41; January, 1964.

Clark, B. P. *Educating the Expert Society.* San Francisco: Chandler Press, 1962.

Combs, Arthur. "Fostering Self-Direction." *Educational Leadership,* 23:373-376; February, 1966.

Counts, George. "Social Understanding for Survival." *Educational Leadership,* 18:485-488; May, 1961.

Cremin, L. A. *The Transformation of the Schools.* New York: Alfred A. Knopf, Inc., 1961.

Crow, Lester D. and Alice Crow. *Adolescent Development and Adjustment.* New York: McGraw-Hill Book Company, Inc., 1965.

Davidson, Helen H. and Gerhard Lang. "Children's Perceptions of Their Teachers' Feelings Toward Them Related to Self-Perception, School Achievement and Behavior." *Journal of Experimental Education,* 29:107-118; December, 1960.

Frandsen, A. N. *Educational Psychology: The Principles of Learning and Teaching.* New York: McGraw-Hill Book Co., Inc., 1961.

Frymier, Jack R. *The Nature of Educational Method.* Columbus, Ohio: Charles E. Merrill Books, Inc., 1965.

Gallagher, James R. *Emotional Problems of Adolescence*. London: Oxford University Press, 1964.

Gallagher, James R. *Medical Care of the Adolescence*. New York: Appleton-Century-Crofts, Inc., 1960.

Havighurst, Robert J. "Do Junior High School Youth Grow Too Fast?" *National Association of Secondary School Principals Bulletin*, 47:161; April, 1963.

Johnson, Mauritz, Jr. "School in the Middle-Junior High: Education's Problem Child," *Saturday Review*, 45:40-42; July 21, 1962.

Kallen, David J. "Inner Direction, Other Direction, and Social Integrative Setting." *Human Relations*, 16:75-87; February, 1963.

Mead, Margaret. "The Young Adult." Reprinted from *Values and Ideals of American Youth*. Edited by Eli Ginzberg. New York: Columbia University Press, 1961.

Mills, G. E. "How and the Why of the Middle Schools." *Nation's Schools*, 68:43-53; December, 1961.

Rice, A. H. "What's Wrong with Junior Highs? Nearly Everything." *Nation's Schools*, 74:30; November, 1964.

Rollins, Sidney and Adolph Unruk. *Introduction to Secondary Education*. Chicago: Rand McNally and Company, 1964.

Trump, J. Lloyd. "Developing a More Dynamic Junior High School Program." *Educational Forum*, 48:129-143; March, 1964.

Waetjen, Walter B. and Robert T. Leeper, eds. *Learning and Mental Health in the School*. Washington, D.C.: Association for Supervision and Curriculum Development, 1966.

Woodring, Paul. "The New Intermediate School." *Saturday Review*, 77-78; October, 1965.

Woodring, Paul and John Scanlon, eds. *American Education Today*. New York: McGraw-Hill Book Company, 1963.

NEW LINCOLN SCHOOL

Knowing
the
Middle School

2

Planning for Middle School

Enrollment in middle school establishes a milestone in the student's educational program. The student enters a new phase of his development different and distinct from his elementary school experiences. The student may have attended school in a relatively pure ethnic neighborhood. While individual persons within the neighborhood may have held varying opinions as to the role that school should play in the child's life, a somewhat general attitude was reflected toward the school throughout the area. Neighborhood children are quite aware of the degree of regard accorded a particular school and they are emotionally conditioned to school by those prevailing attitudes.

A transition to the middle school may cause some concern to the student. The neighborhood elementary school was a familiar and friendly place, located close to his home. He was able to walk to school and to use the school's outdoor area to participate in play, games, and sports during weekends and the summer months. Since the school population was small, he knew most of the other children and the school staff. His closest playmates were in the same school groups as he. He had developed sets of behavioral patterns that related him to the school and gave him self-assurance in the school environment.

Middle school attendance brings many changes. Since the school is no longer within walking distance, some type of transportation must be used. The middle school plant seems large and impersonal compared to the familiar neighborhood school and its inviting play areas. The school population not only is larger, but also is different structurally. The homogeneous ethnic group is replaced by heterogeneity. The population contains children who have only limited acquaintance with children from other races or from different backgrounds. The number of students that the child knows forms a small part of the school population. The physical characteristics of the child appear different—when leaving elementary school he saw himself as being quite grown up in respect to kindergarteners. The middle school population is comprised of boys as tall as the new student's father and girls resembling "grown-up" older sisters. The professional staff contains none of the persons the child knew at the neighborhood school. He wonders if his former behavioral pattern is workable in the new school environment.

A school orientation program for students initially entering middle school is mandatory. Conditions enumerated cause apprehension in the student's mind as to his adequacy to live in the new school environment. The transition program must persuade him that his contributions to the middle school community are going to be important. He must be made to feel that middle school is his school—a place where the student shares responsibility for his growth, where he lives in an environment that encourages originality, creativity, self-expression and inquiry, where success is measured by student progress, and where achievements are recognized. An effective orientation program contributes to a more rapid assimilation into the student team and facilitates teacher team programming for the new students.

A middle school program, as in every type of school, must involve parents as well as students. The school program featuring the following may be new to both students and parents.

1. Non-grade structure where students may progress on a continuous learning basis without recognized grade levels or grade classifications.

2. Student teams composed of various-aged students selected for combination based upon the predicted benefits the students will accrue through interaction with each other and the teaching teams in their educational endeavors.

3. Teaching teams composed of interdiscipline professional staff members integrating their style and talents to provide common support to student team learning situations.

4. Independent study activity through which the student fulfills an obligation he assumes in program planning with the teaching team. Effective independent study requires a motivated student who is willing to undertake whatever activities may be needed to complete the obligation. The nature of the activities are a function of the discipline or specialties area, the students level of proficiency, and resources available.

Parental attitudes toward school and school programs have been conditioned by training received by parents, reading that parents have done, and the general feeling toward education held by particular ethnic groups. The middle school must recognize the existence of parental needs and attitudes. The problem of communication between the middle schooler and his parents was discussed in a previous section.

The more articulate the parent becomes concerning the middle school, the better communication between parent and student can become in this area. Improved parent-student communication contributes to student success during his middle school years.

Parents must understand middle school objectives and operations. The school for its part must understand parental concern for the education of their children. Both must have an appreciation and an understanding of the role each is to play in furnishing learning support to students. The importance of a closed communication loop cannot be overemphasized. An effective communication loop is shown in Figure 2-1.

The closed communication loop portrayed depicts a communication system, sans external signal generators (peer groups, school and community agencies and the like), that exists among the students, parents, and school. During the early school years, the communication link between parents and students tends to be relatively free of noise (interference) and communication between parent and students is good; the communications link (A) between the student and school is weak. The school must rely heavily during these years upon the parent in helping the school to be better informed about the student. The parent occupies an excellent vantage point to modulate the school's communication with the student.

During the student's middle school years, the student experiences the desire for freedom from the parent. The noise level in the communication link between parent and student rises sharply. As this phenomenon occurs, the link A becomes stronger. Middle schoolers tend to form close friendships with adults outside of the home. Teachers may readily become confidants of the students. Now the parent may have to rely heavily upon the school not only for educational development reports, but also for other information about their child. Without the school's inputs to the parent, the channels of communication between the child and parent may become inoperable. When a breakdown occurs, the school stands to lose the parent's ability to modulate effectively communications between school and the student. In extreme cases, the parent may assess the communication problem as being school related; under such circumstances the nominal modulating signal changes to a blocking form. In any case, all parties in the communication network are adversely affected. The importance of good communication among the middle school, parent, and student cannot be overlooked.

Introducing the Student and Parents to Middle School

Preparing the student and parent for inclusion in the middle school environment requires careful planning. The middle school student population represents a cross section of community life as contrasted with neighborhood schools where the probability of homogeneous background is high. Differences will become more discernible in the future when middle schools which are part of the educational plazas envisioned by cities such as East Orange, New Jersey, become operational.

The middle school is an integrator as compared with present junior high schools which also accept students from several neighborhood schools. The task of student/parent middle school introduction is more necessary since the students are arriving at an earlier age. To illustrate the problem using the city of Cincinnati as an example: the downtown areas are populated by low income ethnic groups. When the students leave six-grade elementary schools, they matriculate to junior high schools located within the downtown areas, thus continuing the background patterns that existed in the elementary school on into the junior high school. The new middle schools will preferably be located on large sites so that they are separated from surrounding areas by a "green belt." The middle school will not be associated with any one particular neighborhood, yet it will integrate students from several.

The trend has been a flight of the most prosperous citizenry to the suburbs. Past experience may cause the citizen to

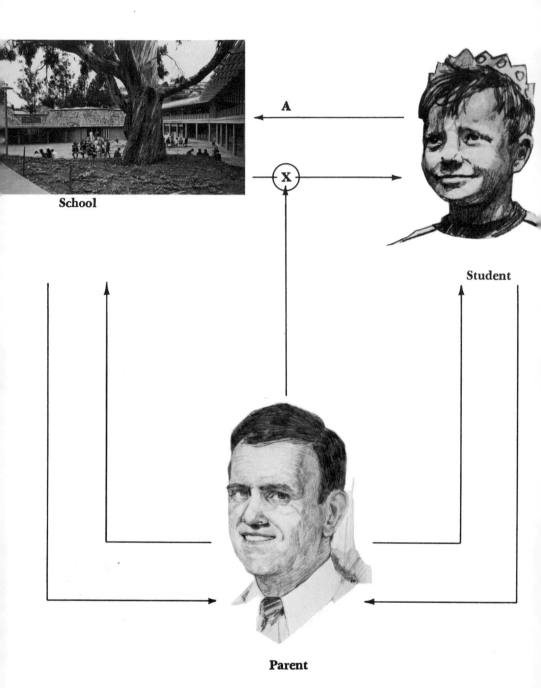

School

A

X

Student

Parent

Figure 2-1 *Communication loop for optimizing parental support of middle school students.*

believe that a high degree of ethnic/economic homogeneity can be maintained in suburban school districts. Beliefs of this nature appear to be invalid considering present conditions. Recent events prognosticate that many marginally financial school districts will be unable to meet their educational obligations in the near term future. School redistricting appears to be the order of the day. Many states are confronted with mammoth redistricting situations. Reliance upon federal funds for school district support will intensify rather than relieve many problems for the local school district since federal school support financing is inherently tied to the provision of equal opportunities for all students.

An effective program for students enrolling in middle school for the first time must create the impression that the individual student counts! He will not be just another name on a record book, but will be known personally by the professional staff members. The manner of assigning students to teams is discussed later. It suffices to mention now that an important part of planning is the selection and assignment of students to teams. Long before the start of the fall school term, letters can be sent to parents advising them of the assignment of the student to a specific team. The use of a "big brother" concept is helpful. The big brother, a student who has been at middle school for two or three years, may call on the incoming new team member and welcome him to the team.

Possibilities for activities to use in conjunction with a first day middle school program are numerous. Among the activities that have proven useful in the past are (a) tours of the middle school plant conducted by members of the student council; (b) use of video tapes or a live panel discussion to inform the newcomers about different features of the middle school program; (c) displays and demonstrations covering projects completed in the disciplines and unified arts; (d) enactment by students and teachers of typical learning situation sequences; (e) demonstration of the use of specialized equipment in the language and skills laboratory, and operation of a portable reception center for both the reception and recording of information; and (f) the functions of the many student activity groups operating in middle school.

It must be stated that a *single day's* program is not likely to accomplish the type of introduction for students and parents that is desired. The introductory day is for stage-setting purposes. It must be neither too superficial in approach as to ignore the differences that exist among students and parents, nor so structured that differences among those attending are accentuated. A possible approach to the program is for the professional staff to plan generally the program activities, which would be in accordance with the objectives to be established through the program, and for the student body to plan many of the details for program inclusion. Some of the more successful introductory day programs have utilized the student council in planning and executing the program. The following example illustrates how a student council may be involved.

One student council began its planning early in the summer. Letters were written and sent to all new students and their parents. Student brochures containing a school map of the plant and tentative introductory day agenda were dispatched with the letters. The student council made name tags for each new student. The new enrollees were grouped into units of ten students each, in accordance with prospective student team membership. Student council members were assigned to act as guides for each of the units. The council member assigned as a guide to a unit was an actual member of the student team to which particular units were assigned. For example, the ten members of a given unit who were tentative team members of Team Z had as a guide a student council member from Team Z. The organizing of new students and their guides for orientation day activities permitted the ten new team members to become acquainted with each other and a veteran team member.

Council made plans for using the auditorium for the program. Place cards throughout the room facilitated seating arrangements for the new members and their parents. Council planned all details for the day and for the execution of all activities. The program planned consisted of the following events:

9:00	Music by the Middle School band and welcome by the student council president who served as presiding officer for orientation day.
9:15	Introduction of student council members, teacher teams and teacher specialists.
9:25	Vice president of the student council discussed the work of the student council and explained how members obtained their offices.
9:45	Student council representatives gave a preview of what it means to be a middle schooler.
10:00	Officers from student activities gave information on the purposes and projects of their respective ventures and additional pertinent information was given.
10:30-11:30	Student guides conducted new students on a tour of the school plant including indoor and outdoor facilities. Panel discussion by council members and staff professionals concerning cardinal features of the middle school program for parents.
11:30-12:30	Luncheon given by the student council for new students. Parents were guided on tours of the school plant.
12:30- 1:30	Panel discussion by council members and staff professionals concerning cardinal features of the middle school program for students. Luncheon sponsored by P.T.A. for par-

ents. Background music presented by the
"Six Strings," a middle school instrumental group.

1:30   Program concluded.

Planning for the prospective middle school parent is a
must to develop proper attitudes toward the middle school
and to prepare the parent to participate in learning situation
support. The day when the parent can be ignored in the
learning situation is past. He is needed and has much to
contribute. A parent with neither an understanding of middle school educational objectives nor an appreciation for the
emphasis on individual programs is a luxury that a middle
school cannot afford. Parental ignorance causes mistrust in
the educational program and may lead to the parent's making extremely unwise decisions to the detriment of his child's
educational welfare. Parental bigotry and shortsightedness
have adversely affected many educational innovations.

Parents are not to be condemned for actions taken because
of ignorance. Life in the United States today places extremely
heavy time demands upon all parents regardless of their
occupational calling. The blue collar worker is as pressed for
efficient time utilization as the white collar or professional
worker. These people no longer have time for thoughtful
reflection concerning the nature of effective educational practices. They are more likely to hark back to their own educational experiences of the 1920's and 1930's to form a frame
of reference for what constitutes an educational program.
Since these people are no longer in step with the times, they
are unable to adjust their thinking to education for the
1970's. In many disciplines, students are already as informed
by their middle school days as their fathers were upon leaving high school.

When parental involvement is discussed, reference is made
to the type of program that will motivate parents to attune
themselves to the middle school of the 1970's. They must

learn how to communicate with their youngsters if the closed learning loop shown in Figure 2-1 is to be effective. It is recognized that parents are like children relative to where to start with a learning program. The individual differences among parents regarding ability to learn are probably greater than those of their children. Age is no magic cure-all for eliminating differences in learning rates. It does little good to develop a standard program for all parents nor to advance all of them at the same rate of progress. Such a concept violates the principles of learning upon which the middle school is predicated.

The program must be individualized to suit the learning capabilities of the parental population. It is not being suggested that parents be put through a thorough diagnostic testing program before initiating a learning program for each, as is the case in some middle school disciplines for students. Rather, what is being suggested is that the middle school staff get to know the prospective parents long before the children are enrolled in middle school. By interview, the parents' level of understanding of the learning process and the middle school objective can be ascertained. The task is not an impossible one. If our recommended middle school size of 700 to 800 students is adopted, and if the school were to have eight student teams, then the parents allotted to each teaching team will be approximately fifty. Considering that a teaching team has five full professionals, a learning coordinator and four teachers, the school task of developing a useful parent program does not seem so monumental.

The teaching team can organize a program for its new parents in accordance with the information learned in the interviews. The last thing to be recommended would be a *common* curriculum for *all* parents. Division of the parents into small groups of 5 to 12 each is recommended with provision for individual study for all parents. The separation into different groups is highly desirable from the group dynamics viewpoint. The groups working with their leaders can determine which aspects about the middle school they wish to study. The following topics are suggested as a guide for group inquiry:

> Importance of Individualized Instruction
> What is Independent Study?
> How an Ungraded School Operates
> Nature of Team Teaching
> Curricula Programming for Given
>   Disciplines
> Preadolescent Psychology
> Learning Theories
> Student Performance Evaluation
> Communications Theory
> School Activities
> Programmed Learning
> The Library/Materials Center Functions
> The Probable Impact of Technology on
>   Education

If the above list looks as if it involves much study by the parent, it has served its purpose. Parent programs will mean work for both parents and the teaching team. The program should not be started on a "catch as catch can" basis. The parental/teaching team groups should establish a schedule and follow it. As parents find that they cannot maintain the schedule, new groups should be formed to handle those who are progressing at a slower learning rate. As a suggestion, it might be possible to combine an evening of middle school discussion with tea and cookies later. Middle schools looking at the need for continual improvement of the quality of education afforded the 10 to 14-year-olds must hasten to initiate a middle school parent program now.

SELECTED READINGS

Anderson, Robert H. "Organizing Groups for Instruction," *Individualizing Instruction,* Sixty-first Yearbook of the National Society for the Study of Education, Part I. Chicago: University of Chicago Press, 1962.

Baynham, Dorsey. "School of Future in Operation," *Phi Delta Kappa,* 42:350-354; May, 1961.

Beggs, David W., III, ed. *Team Teaching—Bold New Venture.* Indianapolis: Unified College Press, Inc., 1964

_____ and Edward G. Buffie, eds. *Independent Study-Bold New Venture.* Bloomington, Indiana: Indiana University Press, 1965.

Byrne, Richard H. *The School Counselor.* Boston: Houghton Mifflin Company, 1963.

Cottingham, Harold F. and William E. Hopke. *Guidance in the Junior High School.* Bloomington, Ill.: McKnight and Mc-Knight, 1961.

DeCecco, John P. *Human Learning in the School.* New York: Holt, Rinehart and Winston, Inc., 1963.

DeHaan, Robert F. *Accelerated Learning Programs.* Washington, D.C.: The Center for Applied Research in Education, Inc., 1963.

Dufay, Frank R. *Ungrading the Elementary School.* West Nyack, New York: Parker Publishing Co., Inc., 1966.

Faunce, Roland C. and Morrell J. Clute. *Teaching and Learning in the Junior High School.* Belmont: Wadsworth Publishing Company, Inc., 1963.

Fine, Benjamin. *Your Child and School.* New York: The Macmillan Company, 1965.

Getzel, J. W. and P. W. Jackson. *Creativity and Intelligence.* New York: John Wiley & Sons, Inc., 1962.

Goodlad, John I. "Individual Differences and Vertical Organization of the School." *Individualizing Instruction,* Sixty-first Yearbook of the National Society for the Study of Education, Part I. Chicago, 1962.

_____ and Robert Anderson. *The Nongraded Elementary School*. New York: Harcourt, World & Brace, Inc., 1963.

Havighurst, Robert L. *Growing Up in River City*. New York: John Wiley and Sons, 1962.

Henry, N. B., ed. *The Dynamics of Instructional Groups*. Fifty-ninth Yearbook of the National Society for the Study of Education, Part II. Chicago: University of Chicago Press, 1960.

Howe, Harold. "The Curriculum, the Team, and the School: An Examination of Relationships." *California Journal of Secondary Education*, 37:353:361; October, 1962.

"Intelligence and Creativeness." *Childhood Education*, Vol. 39, April, 1963.

Johnson, Mauritz, Jr., and others. *Junior High School Guidance*. New York: Harper & Row, Publishers, 1961.

Johnson, Walter F., Buford Stefflre, and Roy A. Edelfelt. *Pupil Personnel and Guidance Services*. New York: McGraw-Hill Book Co., Inc., 1961.

Kelly, Earl C. *In Defense of Youth*. Englewood Cliffs, New Jersey: Prentice-Hall, Inc., 1962.

Kiell, Norman. *The Adolescent Through Fiction*. New York: International Universities Press, Inc., 1959.

_____ *The Universal Experience of Adolescence*. New York: International Universities Press, Inc., 1964.

Kimball, S. T. and J. E. McClellan, Jr. *Education and the New America*. New York: Random House, 1962.

Manlove, Donald C. and David W. Beggs, III. *Flexible Scheduling —Bold New Venture*. Bloomington, Indiana: Indiana University Press, 1965.

Mowrer, O. H. *Learning Theory and Behavior*. New York: John Wiley & Sons, Inc., 1960.

Payne, Donald and Paul Mussen. "Parent-Child Relations and Father Identification Among Adolescent Boys." *Journal of Abnormal and Social Psychology*, 50:358-362; March, 1962.

Quillen, I. James and Lavone A. Hanna. *Education for Social Competence*. Chicago: Scott, Foresman and Company, 1961.

Raths, Louis E., *et al., Values and Teaching*. Columbus, Ohio: Charles E. Merrill Books, Inc., 1966.

Shane, Harold G. "The School and Individual Differences." *Individualizing Instruction,* Sixty-first Yearbook of the National Society for the Study of Education, Part I. Chicago: University of Chicago Press, 1962.

Tobias, Milton. "Disordered Development Is Key to Unlawful Behavior." *Loyola Digest,* p. 5; May, 1963.

Torrance, E. P. *Guiding Creative Talent.* Englewood Cliffs, New Jersey: Prentice-Hall, Inc., 1962.

Trump, J. Lloyd. "Imagines of the Future: A New Approach to Secondary Education." *Urbana Commission on Experimental Study of the Utilization of Staff in Secondary School, National Association of Secondary School Principals Bulletin,* January, 1959.

_____ "Basic Changes Needed to Serve Individuals Better." *Educational Forum,* 26:93-101; November, 1961.

_____ and Dorsey Baynham. *Focus on Change: Guide to Better Schools.* Chicago: Rand McNally, 1961.

Vorobev, G. "Developing Independence and Creativity in Students." *Soviet Education,* 5:41-48; September, 1963.

Wrenn, C. Gilbert. *The Counselor in a Changing World.* The Commission on Guidance in American Schools. Washington D.C.: American Personnel and Guidance Association, 1962.

3

Middle
School
Staff

Introduction

In the middle school an approach to education is formulated that focuses the spotlight upon the learning experience of the individual student. The approach calls for boldness and belief in the new principles of education. Nowhere is courage more necessary than in the selection of the professional staff.

We must search for the persons we want and establish with them the belief that the future for the education of the 10- to 14-year-old resides in the middle school. Specifications for the personnel staff now need to be developed.

Teacher Specifications

Teacher specifications define the personal characteristics of the personnel staff needed for middle school. There is one broad generalization: the middle school teacher must be a person who likes children. How do you identify such a person? No test can select such an individual with a 99.99 per cent level of confidence, but the kind of teacher needed by the middle schooler can be defined. He will enjoy students who are active, energetic, and loud, and will.take teasing in his stride. He will be flexible and sensitive to quick changes of moods and needs, and will sense group feeling and student interaction.

Some examples of the teacher who meet requisites of the middle school staff are presented here:

Profiles of middle school teachers. Miss Olive easily establishes rapport with her students. She evidences quick wit, a happy facial expression, and a calm easy manner. She laughs easily, knows when to talk privately with a student, when to listen, and when to reassure. She contrives situations to permit students to demonstrate newly acquired capacities. Her understanding of students' reactions to situations permits her to anticipate student feeling and behavior. She is a happy individual who radiates enthusiasm for teaching.

Mr. Brown's chronological age is not much greater than that of his students. To him, life and learning are adventures to be diligently pursued—the day is too short to accommodate his activities. Each new learning experience in the middle school is a new adventure. Mr. Brown shares in students' learning discoveries. No detail of the learning experience is too unimportant to relate to him. He listens, he commands, he shares in talking and telling others of learning accomplishments. His smile is contagious to those around him. Mr. Brown does not labor consistently at generating an affection for learning and a stimulating climate; such things just happen when Mr. Brown is around.

Miss May is the idol of the middle school girls. She is a recent college graduate. Physically attractive, she occasionally works as a professional model. Her manner of dress and grooming are widely copied resulting in greater attention to personal appearances by all of the girls. She enjoys participating in after-school activities. Frequently she joins with middle school students at the skating pond, at a concert, or at the malt shop with groups of boys and girls. She takes an active part in community activities. Under her leadership, middle school youngsters manage the "Spring Beautification Company" sponsored by the village. On Saturday, paint brushes and youngsters are at work; flowers are planted and hedges are cut. Miss May receives weekly reports of progress.

Miss Marge is always involved in some type of search. She is resourceful and skillful with her hands, having constructed a cottage at the lake. She has traveled through the interior of Alaska and the islands adjoining southeastern Alaska in search of Indian artifacts. She has taken an expedition to the Upper Amazon River Valley to learn about primitive cultures. Her association with adventure stimulates her students as she communicates her spirit and inquisitiveness to them. Individual student studies in the social and natural sciences have their genesis from Miss Marge's inexhaustible curiosity and encouragement.

Mr. Luchie is a teacher with expectations—he *expects* students to perform up to their capacities. He has expectations for himself, too, one of which is to learn as much as possible about a student. He astonishes students as he greets them on the second day at middle school with comments such as, "Hello Keith, understand you plan to attend West Point." "Good morning, Jack, that's a classy boat you own. How do you manage to keep it looking that way?" "Jim, that swimming meet was great. You have an excellent stroke." How does he know so much? Students refer to him affectionately as Mr. Bird Dog. If a problem arises, Mr. Luchie can always be counted on to say, "You in trouble with your thinking ability? It's only a matter of time and you'll lick the problem." And Mr. Luchie is right. He is always ready to shake the student's hand and say, "Good going there. I knew I could count on you." Mr. Luchie shares the thrill of student achievement. He personally acknowledges all accomplishments and spreads the word or passes the information around: "Have you seen the project Frank is building in the unified arts room? Go take a look—I'm impressed." Or, "Mary, I heard your arrangement for the orchestra is going to be played at the next assembly. Why not tell Helen and Paula about your next musical work?"

Mr. Green, upon an exit interview from a middle school position, had these comments to make: "These kids are driving me wild. They aren't quiet for more than 15 minutes at a time. I find them loud and noisy, lazy and non-cooperative. And their jokes—the jokes are too much." The students when interviewed noted, "Mr. Green was unfair, always picking on somebody and not prepared for the day." They commented further, "Mr. Green never permits us to plan. He follows the same routines daily. He never allows classes to experiment and fails to respect the opinions of the students." The replacement, Mr. Gray, successfully completed Mr. Green's term. Upon his arrival at the middle school Mr. Gray stated, "Hope the students are alive with energy. I loathe students who are conformists and complacent. The students are going to share in decision-making responsibilities. Students' opinions are valuable to me."

Having read the image portraits, the word comes through loud and clear that the middle school teacher must be alive —intellectually, physically and socially. Middle schoolers are growing up, changing, anxious to find themselves—seeking approval, interested in sharing in decision making, and ready to seek solutions to problems through experimentation. The specifications for middle school teachers cannot require less.

Job Specifications

The requirements for special training, experience, and skills have not been defined by any state certification agency or by any of the professional associations. While the most exciting innovation of the latter 20th century grows and develops, those responsible for assuring adequately trained personnel sleep. It may be that the tacit assumption is being made that staffing is not a problem or that the existing supply of elementary and secondary teachers suffices to fill middle school staff requirements. How far from the truth! Junior high school has operated approximately one-half a century under a similar assumption. Only twelve states now issue special certification or endorsement to junior high school teachers, and only a few colleges or universities offer as much as a single course for preparation of the junior high school teacher. The result of this practice is the re-entrance of inadequate high school teachers into the junior high schools.

Training criteria for the middle school teacher. A recent survey failed to find a single institution that provides a curriculum for middle school teacher preparation. The middle school movement cannot assign inadequately prepared elementary, junior and senior high school teachers to its program. Job specifications must be established for middle school teachers. Since specifications are non-existent now, persons or groups must take the initiative in defining their nature. Administrators, along with the College of Education, at the University of Cincinnati, Cincinnati, Ohio, joined forces and conducted the first Middle School Conference in the spring of 1966. This conference along with other small study groups has assisted in crystalizing some job specification criteria. The result of these studies places a premium upon quality middle school staff members. The energetic middle schooler can settle for nothing else.

Consider the three elements that comprise job specification—training, experience and skills. Training is treated but briefly. The minimum training of the middle school staff member is five years in duration or four years (summer sessions included) of college level work culminating in an accredited college degree and a full year of internship in a middle school. Advanced graduate work to support the staff member for his middle school career can best be undertaken after the staff member's aptitude for middle school teaching has been ascertained. The type of experience not only desired but necessary for the middle school staff person is middle school teaching *experience*. An equivalent is the

desire that all prospective commercial airline pilots considered for employment have four-engine jet propelled aircraft experience, when the only possible way to acquire such
experience is to *fly* a four engine jet propelled aircraft. A
possible solution is to recognize equivalent alternative experience. Serving as learning coordinator on a teaching team at
any school level is roughly equivalent to serving on a middle
school teaching team. Non-team teaching experience at either
the elementary or high school level is not equivalent to middle school team teaching. Employment of teachers for middle
school is permissible only after the teachers have served an
appropriate internship period.

The possibility of instituting teaching intern programs
now seems extremely likely. Whereas the practice of student
teaching as now implemented in the several teacher training
institutions in America is clearly suspect, an efficient intern
program in some of the fine middle schools becoming operational in the mid-sixties is a different type of on-the-job
professional preparation. The author has tentatively formulated such a program and will implement it in a middle
school in the near future. The fundamentals of the program
include: (a) the assignment of the neophyte to a teaching
team; (b) participation in student programming with the
teaching team and students; (c) involvement in supporting
students in the learning situation guided by a teaching team
member; (d) participation in small group sessions involving
other neophytes and teaching team group leaders from several disciplines; (e) partaking of staff development activities
along with other professionals; (f) participation in program
formulation, learning how to use the computer to select materials which contribute to the most probable success of individual students in the separate disciplines; (g) taking part
in evaluation conferences with the student, teaching team
and student's parents and serving in various group capacities
as a team of neophytes and professionals pursue projects
leading to the initiation of innovations in the middle school
program. It is stated categorically that the program formulated is intended to establish guidelines within which the

neophyte intern's activities occur. The neophyte meets with the middle school teaching team to which he will be assigned several months before his appointment as an intern. Through a subsequent series of interviews with the intern and discussion with the intern's university instructors, a tentative program is developed. The actual internship program is developed by the neophyte and the teaching team after his arrival at the middle school. The intern's program is formulated using a flow diagram similar to that used by the middle school students. His rate of progress is monitored by the teaching team. The program is intended to fit the intern into the middle school program. The internship need not end with the conclusion of a school year. The training may be continued until the middle school employs the neophyte or the university and middle school agree that the objectives of the middle school internship have been accomplished. The necessity for funding the neophyte training if it extends beyond the student's normal graduation date needs to be considered. The possibility of the intern being employed in his intern program by the middle school is a real one. Public schools have never paid for inducting new personnel into their systems. As the schools strive toward greater quality and status, the requirement for sharing in the expense of training talented recruits in internships must be acknowledged.

Teaching skills. The teaching skills needed are learning support skills. The middle school teacher is not teaching math; he is not teaching Mary; he is not teaching math to Mary. He is providing support to Mary so that she can learn math. Supporting Mary to learn math is quite a different task from teaching math to her. The teacher lends support to Mary in the math learning situation in accordance with his understanding of Mary's learning process. The psychological basis for the supportive learning task rests on the following assumption:

Each student has unique learning processes. The teacher cannot assume that the same learning psychology is applicable for each learner. It behooves the teacher to determine which of the multitudinous psychological theories best describes the manner in which a given student learns. The teacher must adapt his understanding of the pertinent psychology to the learning situation.

Mary enters any learning situation with some probability for making progress which may range from very low to extremely high. Her progress will be determined by her initial learning rates as she continues in the learning situation. The teacher can predict with a high degree of confidence the factors involved which will be the major determinants of Mary's progress rate. Through his understanding of her learning process, he can plan for use of the proper experiences that will optimize her learning rate. This concept for teaching math or any other discipline identifies a student-teacher learning ratio that applies to many learning situations, the one to one—the ratio identified is not the old tutorial one. The relationships between learner and teacher differ significantly in supportive learning. In supportive learning, the persons involved intend to optimize learning in a new area.

Serving as a teaching team member at middle school is going to demand new skills from the professional staff. Not only is the professional going to have to be a walking curricula for his students in his chosen discipline, but also, he is going to have to be a skilled psychologist capable of maximizing learning in all sizes of group situations. He is going to have to be a master in human relations, fully understanding the leadership function and the complexities of how students are motivated. He must develop his communicative skills. Where previously he had few academic encounters with his colleagues concerning the development of a particular student, in the middle school, he will be a part of a team organized to bring to fruition many talents to support the student's growth and development.

The teacher must develop new decision-making capabilities. He is expected to contribute to his student's needs to make rational decisions. He is constantly called upon to decide how progress rates of students in his discipline can be optimized, and he is further challenged to develop new criteria for determining when a given progress rate *has* been optimized. An understanding of decision theory and a working knowledge of the mathematics available to provide data for decision-making must be incorporated into the teacher's repertoire of capabilities.

Middle School Principal

The middle school principal is a middle school manager. His management functions are those of planning, organizing, and controlling. He is the manager to whom the superintendent delegates the responsibility of the middle school operation.

The principal deals with many forces and factors that act upon the school. A force is defined as any influence that impinges upon the school and is capable of materially affecting the nature and scope of the education provided. A factor is described as an element of a force that acts to alter the existing situation. Many examples of forces and factors may be enumerated.

Among the forces acting upon the school are external agencies, people, finance, government legislation, prevailing education philosophy, learning theory, technology, and educational goals to enumerate but a few. Each of the forces may be broken down into factors as was done for the "people" factor in figure 3-1. In fulfilling his managerial functions, the principal must be aware of the forces and factors at work in his school situation at a given time and address himself to them.

The middle school principal's task is much more difficult than that of either the elementary or junior high school principal. The forces affecting the school have long been identified and an equilibrium condition reached with the factors involved. For example, teacher training institutions assiduously turn out teachers capable of performing a reasonably good job in the elementary or junior high school.

The depth of difficulty involved in recruiting and assimilating professionals into the middle school program where innovation strategies are utilized has already been indicated. Figure 3-1 illustrates the major people factors that interrelate with the principal.

Traditionally, principals have emerged from the teaching ranks. A study by the author involving 183 junior high schools in Ohio revealed that 54.7 percent of the principals have been either social studies or physical education teachers. Ninety-one percent possess at least a master's degree in education. The background of the principal suggests that the future middle schools will have a problem in recruiting an adequate supply of managers in the near term future. The middle school principalship requires persons with broad educational and managerial experience and training. An intern program for principals is a predicted necessity.

The planning function. Planning starts with the development of a set of objectives—some are near-term and some long-term; some can be accomplished easily while others require the assumption of a higher degree of risk. The middle school principal begins his planning within the framework of policies and objectives established by the school board and superintendent. His objectives too are both short- and long-term. He delineates the activities required to accomplish his objectives, and establishes the resources required to carry out the activities. Almost all of the planning that is done in the middle school involves many people.

The effective principal delegates part of the planning function to his staff. He makes it clear to them, however, that final planning decisions rest with him. Those most vitally involved with planning are students, staff, parents and community.

The middle school with its emphasis on team teaching results in much of the planning for the student being done by the teaching teams. The principal, counselor-teachers, and learning coordinators have regular staff meetings to discuss future plans and to modify current operational plans as re-

Parents

Students

Professional Staff

Other Principals

School Superintendent

Middle School Principal

Community

Other Agencies

P.T.A.

Figure 3-1 *People factors in middle school environment inter-relating with principal.*

quired. Detailed planning within the teaching teams concerning students is discussed fully in Chapter 4.

In the special area, the principal plans for the student. He meets with his staff members concerned with the unified arts, health and physical education skills, language laboratories, electronic center and the library. Planning with these staff members involves an understanding of equipment features utilized. Long lead times are involved in making equipment changes, and more emphasis is placed on long term planning. In this area, planning will become more critical as electronic technological contributions to the middle school increase in scope and complexity.

The principal plans for student activities through the students. The middle school is the school of change, of growing up naturally, of discovering one's self, and of inquiry. It is a school that adapts to its students' requirements. The middle school has many activities in which students can participate and can also share in planning. The student activities are discussed in Chapter 2.

The principal plans for organizational activities. Many community and school-related organizations make use of middle school plant facilities. The school discussed in Chapter 5 incorporates features especially designed to facilitate community use of school facilities. Planning must be done to accomplish the objectives of community facility use and still minimize the effects of such use upon the middle school program.

Some organizations like the Parents Teachers Association (P.T.A.) are co-partners with the staff in implementing the middle school program. The P.T.A. is a good resource to use, since its chief contribution is the work of interested people. Through effective planning, one middle school and the P.T.A. were able to develop a P.T.A. nucleus that performed bountiful service in preparing a community for the initiation of cogent aspects of a middle school program.

The principal plans with his superintendent, his professional staff, consultants, and architects for future middle school plant facilities. Facility planning now is a continuous function instead of the once-in-a-lifetime situation of prior years. The middle school, which provides for a school ever responsive to students' changing needs, calls for anticipatory planning to be done. Reference is made in Chapter 5, dealing with the school plant, to the need for keeping an architect on a retainer fee to plan with the appropriate school personnel for facility changes.

A number of planning areas in which the principal participates has been discussed. None is more important than the one about to be considered—"Staff Growth and Development." Professional staff growth and development is imperative to the middle school. Merely to supply competent personnel on a continual basis to the middle school is inadequate. The middle school staff is spoken of as *being* the curricula. A staff can become obsolete as well as any other middle school resource. Technological change rate is such that data becomes obsolescent in less than a decade. For example, in the electronics field, transitors were the excitement in the 50's, replacing the bulky, unreliable vacuum tubes in power amplifying circuits. Transitors are giving way in the 60's to solid state chips which can be packaged in much smaller units with an ultimately greater life, lower power requirement, and higher reliability. A plan is required that encourages the middle school staff to continue to be experts in their respective disciplines, as well as in the social sciences which are so essential to the support of learning. Staff motivation for self-improvement has a positive correlation with the principal's planning of activities for the staff's growth and development. An appropriate, short account is illustrative of the fact. The principal's former position was filled from within the school system's personnel. A member of the middle school professional staff stated: "Staff inspiration is falling off rapidly. No longer is there a source of energy emerging from the principal's office that glows through the school and motivates the staff to use all our existing capacities to the utmost and to search diligently for new learnings that will enable the staff to elevate itself to an ever increasing level of aspiration."

The school atmosphere is the result of many tangible and intangible factors. A stimulating atmosphere results from conscientious planning by the principal and staff. The principal can plan his activities in such a way that he will be available to his staff when required. Through his knowledge of the staff's capabilities, he can "arrange" to be present when the teaching team needs that extra person to accomplish an objective. He can plan activities that will motivate the staff to congregate at a given place in the school day. One middle school principal became a coffee chef presiding at the coffee maker before 0800 every day. Thus the morning "coffee" achieved the cross conversation desired among the professional staff.

The principal should plan to praise his staff. Yes, plan! Psychologically, the principal is on sound ground when planning to implement a program that requires him to acknowledge outstanding work wherever it is observed. Industry has long recognized the impetus that praise has upon the staff. The Martin Company, a defense contractor, instituted an award program for work free from errors. The result was a significant increase in error-free performance. The program proved so successful that it has spread throughout the Air Force in a form known as "Zero Defects."

The nature of the middle school requires that the principal delegate responsibility to the various teaching teams that he previously retained for himself. The professionalism of the teaching team is stressed. As professionals they must be afforded the opportunity to make decisions relative to factors impinging upon their particular student teams. The principal, to be sure, has the residual responsibility for the overall effectiveness of middle school, but daily decisions involving the teaching team should be made at that level. For example, the teaching team must be permitted to make decisions regarding specific student programs, decisions about

activities among team members, utilization of material resources allocated to them, student progress evaluation, and
factors of a similar nature. The delegation of such responsibility by the principal will strengthen rather than weaken
his position with the staff. Not only will the staff have the
opportunity for professional development through the decision-making process, but the principal will be afforded time
for conceptualizing broad courses of action that will insure
the continuing improvement of middle school education.

A device has been developed in Figure 3-2 to enable the
principal to evaluate his practices relative to the delegation
of responsibility. A fundamental management principle
states that the necessary authority and resources to carry out
the task must be delegated with the responsibility. The grid
is laid out in arbitrary units with authority shown on the
coordinate and decision activities laid out on the abscissa.
Four levels of principal and staff activities relative to decision making are identified ranging from decisions announce-
ment by the principal to decision-making by the staff. The
range of decision-making then ranges from principal centered
to staff centered. Ideally, the middle school principal should
find his decisions-making practices lying well to the right
hand side of the grid.

Organization. The organizational function of the middle
school principal is to combine the resources available in a
manner which will enable middle school objectives to be
accomplished in an efficient and economical manner.

The principal must be guided by the flexibility tenet of
the middle school in formalizing his organizational structure.
Accepted organization patterns may be followed, but only if
they do not conflict with flexibility. *Flexibility does not mean
instability.* Flexibility is the characteristic of an organization
which enables it to accommodate changes in factors impinging upon the school without necessitating major changes in
organization structure. The organization formulated must be
able to account for changing requirements without disrup-

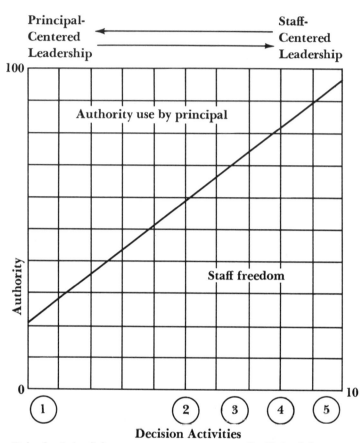

Principal-
Centered
Leadership

Staff-
Centered
Leadership

Authority use by principal

Staff freedom

Authority

Decision Activities

Principal Activity	Staff Activity
1. Announces decision	No share
2. Makes tentative decision subject to change	No share— participate in discussion only
3. Presents problems—gets suggestions—makes decision	Suggests activity
4. Establishes decision-making limits	Make decision
5. None; decision limits defined by superintendent	Make decision

Figure 3-2
Continuous Range of Leadership Conduct.

tion of normal operations. The use of learning coordinators as nominal team leaders in lieu of assistant principals should be strongly considered.

Two new functions not previously considered in the school organization are the materials center director and public relations director. The requirements for materials increase severalfold when supportive learning replaces teacher centered activities. The acquisition and preparation of required materials cannot be adequately accomplished by other staff members.

The public relations function must be staffed to free the principal from the necessity of devoting large amounts of his time to visiting with parents, visitors and others in the community. The worthwhileness of having the principal devote time for visitation is not to be discounted, but the press of other responsibilities, especially in the planning areas, makes the inclusion of a public relations expert on the staff mandatory.

Controlling. The controlling function of the principal is broken down into three aspects: predicting how well performance is going to be, measuring actual performance, and taking corrective action. Controlling involves all aspects of the middle school program. It contributes to the effectiveness of the staff growth and development program.

The usual criteria for measuring successful operation of an enterprise are schedule, cost, and technical performance. Education has tended to ignore the cost and schedule evaluation facets and to rely heavily upon technical performance evaluation. Unfortunately, the tools for that evaluation are quite poor. Test scores of students have often been accepted as the principal evidence of performance. Other means for analyzing technical performance must be found.

Program costs generally are related to dollars per student per annum. Available cost information provides only a comparison with other school systems of similar type per pupil. It provides no indication of the cost involved to achieve particular school objectives or student learning.

Schedules provide no meaningful basis for analysis. With state requirements established in terms of number of periods per week per year for a given subject, instruction is geared to the distribution of a certain amount of study material over the requisite time period. Whether the time is too long or too short for particular students to accomplish the subject purposed is not considered.

The controlling criteria—schedule, cost, performance—can be implemented in middle school. The middle school, being organized along responsibility center lines (the teaching-student team) has natural accountability units. The learning coordinator and his teaching team can be held accountable for accomplishing delegated tasks. Since the tasks are job oriented, it is possible to predict performance against a given task and to measure actual against predicted results and to analyze the causes for variances against predicted performance.

The tasks delegated to the teams fall into a number of general categories. Typical categories and related tasks are shown in Figure 3-3. It is not intended that every middle school will utilize the same categories and tasks for control purposes. The principal and his professionals should develop categories and tasks to conform to the characteristics of their particular situation.

The principal and his individual teams will have to agree upon predicted team performance in both quantitative and qualitative terms. They will have to agree, as well, upon how actual performance is to be measured. The predicted performance must be related to a schedule for significant event accomplishments (milestones) and may not necessarily be restricted to a given school year. The cost to achieve the given performance should be estimated. Teaching resources are not free—they must be included as an element of computed program cost.

The principal should hold periodic reviews of team performance. While teaching resources will have to be expended to organize a presentation in flip chart form, the values from

Category	Task
Student growth	optimize growth rate of each student
Independent study	optimize student participation in independent study activity
Learning support	optimize staff support to the student in the learning situation
Small groups	improve effectiveness of staff in small group situations
Curricula	improve capabilities of team members in specific disciplines and social science area
Materials	optimize processes for acquisition and evaluation of materials
Technical innovation	improve team understanding of how technical innovations can be utilized in the middle school program
Scheduling	improve utilization of individual teacher resources through more effective scheduling of teacher activities
Activities	optimize involvement of team with middle school student activities
Middle School planning	optimize effectiveness of team participation in middle school planning
Parents and Community	optimize team relationships with parent and community groups

Figure 3-3 *Categories and tasks involved in evaluating teaching team performance.*

such review makes the effort worthwhile. An analysis of the material presented will enable the principal to determine tentative courses of corrective action to take, if he should find it necessary.

All teaching teams must be present at the reviews. Since the middle school staff time is completely filled during the week, the practice of reviewing on Saturday might be considered. The custom of combining a Saturday review with subsequent social activity has proven successful in some commercial companies.

It is suggested that the principal might organize review teams composed of a cross-section of teachers from individual teaching teams. The review teams would spend two weeks annually with a teaching team to observe activities being carried out and report their findings to the principal. The teacher team subject to the review would be afforded copies of the review team findings. The practice has much to recommend it. The review gives each member of a teaching team the opportunity to participate in an evaluation of another team, and allows the teacher to see how his counterpart in a given discipline is performing on a day-by-day basis. The review team reports give the principal another tool for evaluating the performance effectiveness of his teaching teams.

Although this discussion has dealt exclusively with the principal and his control function as related to the teaching teams, it is not intended to imply that such control activities are the totality of such a function. The principal must continually be aware of his responsibility for performance prediction, actual performance measurement, and for taking corrective action relative to all aspects of his middle school program.

Staffing the Middle School

The middle school staff, professional and paraprofessionals, form a community of people dedicated to the proposition that educating our 10 to 14 year olds is one of America's most challenging and rewarding opportunities.

Selection of each of the community members is important. If we have unwittingly dwelt upon the professional staff, relative to fulfilling auxiliary functions, the intention was not to minimize or exclude the role of the paraprofessionals. We recognize that they are essential to the middle school program.

Special areas. Special areas are made up of the learning and language skills laboratories, unified arts, health and physical education activities, and special interests. The recommended allocation of staff resources for the teaching areas is given in Chart 3-4.

Teaching teams. The 700 to 800 students in middle school are assigned to teaching teams composed of 90 to 100 girls and boys, upon their enrollment. The learning coordinator serves as team leader. Other assigned team members report to him, as administrator except for the counselor-teacher who is assigned functionally. The counselor-teacher is assigned administratively to the principal because he serves two teams. The principal delegates the required responsibility and authority necessary for accomplishing team tasks. The counselor-teacher assists the team with student guidance, parental relations, testing activities and generally fills in where needed on the team.

The establishment of group rapport is paramount to the successful operation of a teaching team. An understanding of the fundamentals of group dynamics is *sine qua non* for prospective members. Team members must share in the appointment of additional or replacement personnel. Contrariwise, a team member who cannot work with the other team members must be removed from the team as expeditiously as possible.

Special staff. The special staff consists of specialists whose jobs enable the school to accomplish more adequately its mission. The materials center specialist is the head librarian. The 20th century has witnessed a proliferation of materials. With its emphasis upon individual study and small group learning situations, the middle school has an insatiable re-

TEACHING AREA	SPECIALTY	QUANTITY
Language skills laboratory	French Spanish Others	4
Learning skills laboratory	Reading Mathematics	3
Unified arts	Art Music Domestic Science Woodworking Ceramics Other technical	8
Health and physical education	Individual Physical proficiency Sports and games	4
Special interest	Typing Journalism Other	5

Figure 3-4 *Allocation of teaching area staff resources for 700-800 student middle school.*

quirement for materials. The materials center must assume a position that will meet the information challenge. The specialist in this job is called upon to devise a system for procuring, cataloguing, storing and retrieving materials of all media. This specialist has technological assistance for operating the electronic center and the associated portable reception centers to maximize their effective usage. With such assistance, the materials center specialist processes—for incorporation into the center—school-produced materials that are used to improve program effectiveness.

The middle schools need paraprofessionals, since professional staff is under constant pressure to improve its contributions to the learning situation. Professional resources must be used as economically and efficiently as possible. The use of the professional can be enhanced through the use of paraprofessionals who bring their special talents to the instructional program and lend assistance in the total middle school program. The materials center has such assistants for compiling and researching materials. Paraprofessionals are also used as laboratory assistants in the science and skills laboratories. They prepare equipment and material for student use and give assistance to individual students who are working in the area where the paraprofessionals are the most knowledgeable.

Using paraprofessionals is an intriguing idea that offers great potential middle school benefits. They are a prime resource that lends support to any program.

SELECTED READINGS

Ashton-Warner, Sylvia. *Teacher.* New York: Simon and Schuster, 1963.

Battrick, Delmer H. "How Do Team Teaching and Other Staff Utilization Practices Fit into the Instructional Program of a Junior High School." *National Association of Secondary School Principals Bulletin,* 46:13-15; October, 1962.

Beggs, David W., III. *A Practical Application of the Trump Plan.* Englewood Cliffs, New Jersey: Prentice-Hall, Inc., 1964.

Bennis, W. G., and D. D. Benne, and R. Chin. *The Planning of Change: Readings in the Applied Behavioral Sciences.* New York: Holt, Rinehart and Winston, 1961.

Berry, John R. "Does Professional Preparation Make a Difference?" *Journal of Teacher Education,* 13:386-395; December, 1962.

Campbell, Roald F., *et al. The Organization and Control of American Schools.* Columbus, Ohio: Charles E. Merrill Books, Inc., 1965.

Carter, William L., *et al. Learning to Teach in the Secondary School.* New York: The Macmillan Company, 1962.

Cunningham, Luvern L. "Keys to Team Teaching." *Overview,* 1:54-55; October, 1960.

Grooms, M. Ann. "The Junior High School Principal's Role in Staff Development in Ohio Schools," Unpublished Doctor's Dissertation, University of Cincinnati, 1963.

Gross, Neal and Ward S. Mason, and Alexander W. McEachern. *Exploration in Role Analysis.* New York: John Wiley & Sons, Inc., 1958.

Misner, Paul J. and Frederick W. Schneider, and Lowell G. Keith. *Elementary School Administration.* Columbus, Ohio: Charles E. Merrill Books, Inc., 1964.

Osborn, Alex F. *Applied Imagination.* New York: Charles Scribner's Sons, 1963.

Parnes, Sidney J. and Harold F. Harding, eds. *A Source Book for Creative Thinking.* New York: Charles Scribner's Sons, 1962.

Polos, Nicholas C. *The Dynamics of Team Teaching.* Dubuque: William C. Brown Company Publishers, 1965.

Singer, Ira S. "Survey of Staff Utilization Practices in Six States." *National Association of Secondary School Principals Bulletin,* 46:1-13; January, 1962.

Skinner, B. F. "Why Teachers Fail." *Saturday Review,* 80-81, 98-102; October, 1965.

Middle School Program Aspects

4

Planning the Curricula

A paramount objective of the middle school is to further the self-development of its students in the several academic disciplines, study skills, problem analysis, and problem-solving areas. Programmed activities are required to accomplish the objectives. To guide middle school planners in their program formulation, a number of premises concerning the middle schools are predicated. Planned activities and events that lie beyond the premises are eliminated after consideration and investigation. They are purposely made general to stimulate the ingenuity of professionals and still furnish program stability. The middle school premises serving as guides to programing are the following:

The worth of the individual student. Certainly the uniqueness of each student must be considered and his opinions and contributions respected and honored. Otherwise how else can the student generate a self-image that is acceptable to himself? The middle school creates the nurturing climate required to permit the development of self-reliant attitudes and confident approaches to problem formulation and decision-making.

Self-determination of the student in the learning environment. The learning environment can be contrived to produce or shape learning but the student becomes a partner in his own success, accepting the responsibility for learning. He should be neither coerced nor cajoled into taking action. His determination for future learning should rest in his own hands. The middle school must provide the learning support required for self-determination in backing up decisions.

Student involvement with change. Change is a way of life in the middle schools. As childhood is left behind and early adolescence approaches, student needs change from security to love, affection, and self-realization. Middle school planning must acknowledge the existence of change and provide for it. Provision for this must be made in such a manner that the student can discover himself, his peers and his physical-socio-economic environment, and relate the discovery to his past cultural heritage as well as to a projection forward into the world of tomorrow.

Decision-making is a natural facet of the growing-up process. The middle school places high value upon self-determination and worth of the student. When such value is established, the assumption is that the student has the capability for making his decision known and the opinion stated. To make a rational determination requires the ability to define the problem, treat it in a scientific manner, and to select an optimum solution within the problem restraint bounds. The middle school must provide its students with access to the tools for decision-making and offer opportunities for developing decision-making skills.

Learning situations—singular and groups. The middle school does not follow a monolithic approach to the learning situation. While individualized learning is paramount, the learning situation may involve group activities as well as the one-to-one relationship. In group situations, uniform standards of achievement are not sought for all students. The group is utilized not because its method of instruction is considered to be a more economical or efficient means for providing education, but because the group situation offers students those learning opportunities beyond the scope of one-to-one relationships. Students have the chance to gain confidence in decision-making capability through comparison of their problem approaches with those of their peers. Group situations afford the means for broadening conceptualization and for crystallizing thoughts.

Growth is discernible. Students begin to mature into pre- or early adolescents during their middle school enrollment periods. The manner in which the changes occur can be observed, recorded and possibly measured, when adequate measuring devices are available or can be constructed. Changes having casual relationships or those which can be directly associated with the middle school plan are identified as criteria within the restraint levels prevailing; the effectiveness of the middle school can be ascertained by reviewing criteria changes related to a specific student. Decision-making skills and mathematical and communication capabilities may be among the criteria to be developed for a given student. By reviewing student documentary data for initial criteria level, changes from the given levels can be observed. Inferences can be drawn concerning student progress, need for changing the curriculum, need for auxiliary study, and effectiveness of the middle school per student resource expenditure. Unless the curriculum does include provision for student growth evaluation, it is only partially complete.

Middle School Curricula

We speak of the middle school curricula for each middle school student as learning programs at a given point in time. The content of the curricula differs from the traditional elementary and junior high schools. Elementary and junior high school curricula are constituted of subject matter placed there for such reasons as difficulty of content, state requirements, textbook writers, tradition, and opinions of curriculum committees. The result of these curricula practices tends to be a fragmented collection of content with individual parts of the curricula becoming ends in themselves. The matter is presented, studied, evaluated, and grades recorded to indicate student exposure to particular content without clear-cut objectives being achieved for the total curriculum.

The curriculum in the middle school is designed to accomplish the long-range objectives of fostering the spirit of inquiry and development of problem analysis/decision-making capabilities. The particular content of the curricula is *that content which the students and professional staff members working with the students determine.* The rapid accumulation of data today makes it inadvisable to concentrate upon the learning of factual information whose usefulness has a limited life expectancy. Rather, the emphasis must be placed upon stimulating the student to investigate the various disciplines, to question what he finds, to conceive new approaches to persistent problems, to evaluate proposed courses of action, and to decide which direction technological, political, economic, and social developments should take.

The middle school attempts to encourage the growth of individualism through returning to America's students a part in determining their educational programs. When the child

enters middle school, he should have acquired some proficiency in the three "R's." The student is ready to participate in his curriculum planning. To be sure, during his early
days at middle school the professionals will exercise con-
siderable influence upon the student's program direction.
However, as the student continues in middle school, ever
increasing responsibility for selecting where his learning efforts will be focused rests upon the student. The student
decides where his inquiry leads him.

The curricular frame of reference for middle school is
composed of the four disciplines: social science, science,
mathematics, and language arts. Also included are the con-
comitant areas such as unified arts, foreign language, music,
and physical education. Within the disciplines, there is no
formal breakdown into courses such as science 6, 7, 8, and 9,
or topics restricted by age of students or number of years in
school. Each discipline is an entity that can be studied from
many aspects; for example, hygiene, physical and natural,
is an aspect of science. Note, these are not divisions but
merely a classification useful for discipline structuring purposes. The professional staff members organize their disciplines so that students can identify and work toward the
accomplishment of management tasks. The staff—utilizing its
own expertise and availing itself of the findings of the many
discipline experts now engaged in determining the elixir of
their specialities—formulates learning programs adaptable
to the learning situation requirements of the individual student.

The middle school finds many practices and activities of
the traditional schools incongruous with its objectives. Included among the unacceptable practices and activities are
self-contained classrooms, the use of professionals to teach
one or two subjects such as seventh grade geography, disre-
gard of individual student interest, use of grades as motivation, acceptance of fact regurgitation as evidence of learning,
and interscholastic athletics. Other nonacceptable practices
and activities can be identified, but the delineation of an

exhaustive list serves no substantial purpose. The essence of the matter is that middle school practices and activities do differ from the other schools. Practices and activities in the middle school are discussed throughout the book. Details of program structure and organization in a number of middle schools are afforded in sequential paragraphs.

Fox Lane Middle School. The staff at Fox Lane implements a unified arts program that offers homemaking, woodworking, ceramics, fine arts and music. The work of students flows through all five disciplines as a project is pursued. Teaching teams are composed of professionals from each discipline. Planning is a mutual experience between students and team members. Opportunities are provided for students to work on projects of personal interest. The accompanying photograph shows some of the girls at work in the unified arts center.

Since the teaching team is concerned with the problem of those students who tend to work exclusively in the areas of highest interest, the staff at Fox Lane has found it necessary to require students to have some experience in each discipline. To further stimulate participation in other disciplines, the staff strives to develop many suggested activities that require work in all areas.

The unified arts program at Fox Lane seeks to provide broad exploratory experiences rather than levels of skills in limited areas. In the unified arts program, students enjoy the thrill of exploring the areas of beauty, creativity and reality without the pressure of tomorrow. By the existence of a permissive environment, students change from being reluctant to show art work because of possible ridicule to being eager to have their work displayed or placed in an art festival. They develop a willingness to talk about what they see or feel in a particular piece of their work. Art becomes something to discuss and to share with others both in and out of school.

Each child has his place in the program, and progresses at

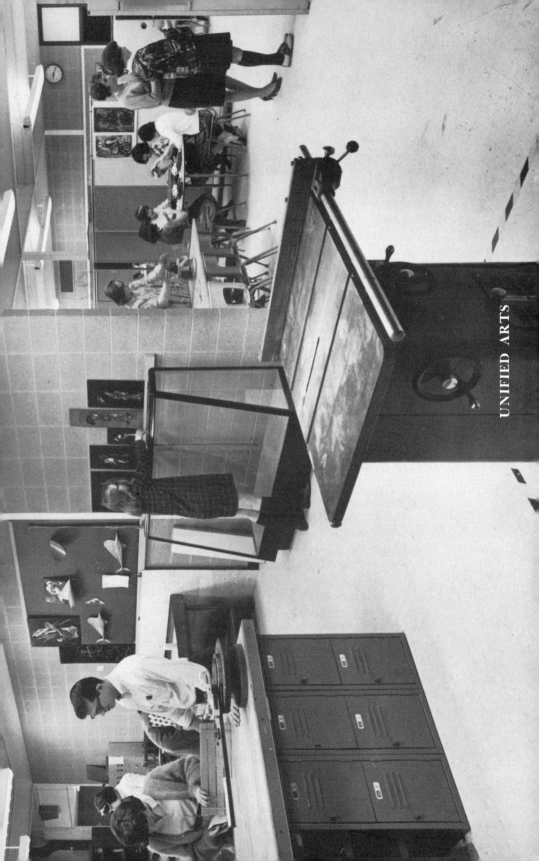

UNIFIED ARTS

his own rate. He is permitted to work in an atmosphere free from the pressure to keep up with other students.

The Fox Lane program is directed toward the individual. No attempt is made to keep the students in groups who share similar ability or interest. The individual is the relevant *one* for instructional purposes.

Valley Green Middle School. Valley Green has a unique mathematical program which features team teaching, ungrading and individualized instruction for its 800 students in the nominal 10 to 14-year-old age group. No mathematics curriculum exists in the traditional sense. For example the curriculum, or rather curricula, for a given year cannot be written down precisely between the covers of a document entitled "Mathematics, Grades 5-8." Curricula evolve as the capabilities and skills of the students are determined. The tentative curriculum is composed by talented members of a professional mathematics team.

Mathematical instruction at Valley Green begins at the existing level of a student's accomplishments. When a new student enters the school, a series of diagnostic inventories are given to determine his abilities in such subject matter as addition, subtraction, multiplication, division, algebra, geometry, and related items. The school needs to ascertain where the student stands relative to a topic. Several days later after the inventory is completed, team members analyze the results to determine possible programs that might be formulated for the student.

Formulation of a student program does not follow immediately from determination of test results—in fact, it is not formulated until the team members and the student have had an opportunity to know one another. It is in this particular area that Green Valley is different from other schools. Determining a student's capabilities in a given discipline can be fairly readily accomplished with the analytic devices available today.

An anecdote, concerning a Valley Green student, is indicative of the necessity for consideration of auxiliary factors when formulating student programs if student cooperation is to be assured. When John entered Valley Green, he was 13 years old, 6'0" tall and weighed almost 200 pounds. He was well-liked by his peers, but displayed an indifferent attitude toward school. Mathematical diagnostic testing revealed capabilities about equivalent to those of an entering 10-year-old. The professional mathematical team to which John was assigned questioned the validity of his test scores. The team therefore recommended that a detailed program be temporarily delayed. Finding that John had established rapport with a science teacher, an arrangement was made for the teacher to utilize John's abilities during the period previously designated for math. Through his science work, John soon realized that a knowledge of arithmetic and algebra were essential to progress in science. He established contact with his mathematical team which had received reports from the science teacher concerning John's increasing interest in math. The team encouraged John to go through diagnostic testing once more. The results were quite different from the original test scores. The staff was able to confidently develop an initial math program. John could now work in this program with the feeling that the activities involved were developed particularly for him. And, you know—John was right.

The preparation of math programs is a major task for the several math teaching teams. The magnitudes of the task arise from the requirement to tailor math programs to fit capabilities of individual students. A logical framework is developed to cover the middle school math objectives, but fine differences in depth and concept, based upon individual capabilities, necessitate program individualization for each student. The task calls for teachers who are highly qualified in mathematical knowledge, possessed of extraordinary understanding of the learning process, and more than willing to accept the challenge of the toughest of programming tasks.

Curriculum content at Green Valley consists largely of self-study materials. The student works alone using such study aids as work sheets, individual texts, programmed books, taped lessons played on cartridge-loading type tape recorders, and disc record players. The photograph shows two middle school students working independently on their math programs.

The student is assisted by the teaching team during his individual study. As blocks are encountered in pursuing the learning program, the team prepares supplementary routines that provide additional experience in the problem area, seeks to help the student find alternate approaches to combat learning difficulties, and conducts group sessions involving both large and small numbers of students when significant problems are encountered.

The math curricula at Valley Green make student progress monitoring mandatory, in order to ascertain the *rate* of progress. Opportunities for progress monitoring are many: during the frequent student-teacher conferences, from evaluation of student analytical ability by teaching teams in the science and social studies areas, and through a rigorous diagnostic testing program. Diagnostic testing instruments are composed of both staff and commercial types.

A further benefit accrues from the monitoring process in terms of effect upon the professional staff. At Valley Green teachers are guides. When the student fails to make recognizable progress toward a designated goal, the teacher guide and the student should both shoulder the responsibility. This is the feeling maintained by the administrative and professional staff at middle school. Consequently, when the rate of student progress reaches a plateau or perhaps even declines, the effectiveness of the learning program for that student becomes suspect. The professional staff is obligated to review carefully the learning program involved and to ascertain what factors can be changed to improve program worth to the student.

Belle Vista. Foreign language instruction at the Belle Vista Middle School *extends* the communicative capabilities of the students—it is not an "extra." The need to communicate

INDEPENDENT STUDY IN MATH

more effectively becomes more stringent with each new break-through in transportation technology. The development of supersonic transport makes all regions of the earth accessible within a matter of hours. Middle school students will have the opportunity for travel never dreamed of by previous generations. The middle schooler needs to be aware of the changing nature of his physical-economic world—to be given the opportunity to determine whether he wishes to broaden his communicating capability, or to restrict himself in this respect. He should be helped to see that self-imposed limitations on information exchange can well be serious obstacles for future career opportunities.

At Belle Vista, foreign language instruction helps the students' audiolingual mastery of the language they choose. Languages offered are not restricted to the common classical ones. Learning is based upon the premise that the first phase of the learning of language is verbal—speaking the language and listening to it as it is spoken by persons with well modulated voices that pronounce words and enunciate syllables in the manner deemed to be correct in the foreign language country. The accompanying photograph shows several students listening in a foreign language study to the language of interest to them. Sound is provided through the media of tapes, cartridges and records. The potential for the studio as a foreign language instructional device is self-evident.

The foreign language curriculum at Belle Vista, and the math curriculum at Valley Green, consists of as many individual curricula as there are students participating. The broad curriculum framework provides a sequential program covering the four-year middle school period. Students entering the program at any time begin where their capabilities permit. Curriculum content includes audio tapes, film strips, cartridges, readers, texts, teacher-generated materials, and visiting linguists.

At Belle Vista, there was a student who had spent several years with his parents in South America and who spoke

LANGUAGE LABORATORY

flawless Spanish. He served as a small group instructor and produced many recordings and tapes that were used by fellow students in their individual learning programs.

The rewards of language learning sometimes occur much earlier to middle schoolers than anticipated. One Belle Vista student, after spending approximately one year in a Spanish curriculum where the audio-lingual approach was accentuated, decided to switch to a French program. Recently he spent a summer in Europe and discovered that he could converse in both languages. Upon his return to school, he related the experience to his fellow students with great enthusiasm. It can be anticipated that similar travel opportunities will be available to increasing numbers of middle schoolers in future years.

A Midwest Middle School Begins

A growing community in a midwestern state decided to open a middle school. Its school district was composed of a high school and several elementary schools. When the policy-makers decided to build a new high school, the old building became a regional school housing grades five through eight and was designated as a middle school. The planning which followed placed grades five and six in self-contained class-rooms and departmentalized grades seven and eight. Special subject teachers and a counselor were provided to assist the teachers in grades five and six. The building contained facilities for physical education, industrial arts, home economics and a science laboratory. The professional staff was composed of former elementary teachers who taught the self-contained classrooms plus those who had taught grades 7 and 8 in the former high school.

After one year at middle school, the staff felt that by combining resources it could do a better job of teaching. Before embarking upon this new venture, the staff prepared a detailed plan composed of the following:

Familiarization with literature discussing team teaching and non-graded schools.

Visits to schools where team teaching could be observed.

Attendance at university conferences dealing with team teaching and non-graded schools.

Invitation of consultants to the school to work with the staff in large/small group situations and in individual conferences. Consultants were provided for the following topics:

> Team teaching
> Individualized Reading
> New English Program
> Developing Social Studies Programs
> How to Use Texts
> Climate for Creativity
> Individualizing Instruction
> Organizing for Learning

The plan was carried out over several months. After the meetings with the consultants, the staff held a series of meetings to discuss ideas about team teaching and non-grading. The meetings disclosed that:

Some professional staff members were afraid to depart from their current modes of teaching.

Some staff members preferred to take a passive role until they had an opportunity to observe fellow staff members working in teaching team and non-grade situations and were able to evaluate activity results.

Some staff members straddled the fence. They suggested that a limited course of action be followed re team teaching and non-grading. Activity should be restricted to a few tryout areas.

Some staff members became avid middle school concept disciples through participating in planned activities. These staff members advocated the use of interdiscipline team teaching and non-grading in all school areas.

What had the look of an impasse situation was quickly resolved by the assistance of staff professionals skilled in group dynamics techniques. Through their efforts negotiations were effected that eventually resulted in three-fourths of the professional staff members joining teaching teams and dedicating themselves to the formulation of curricula framework.

While the professional staff was orienting itself to the middle school, activity was proceeding swiftly in another area where people play a vital role. The P.T.A. was the vehicle used to prepare the community for the initiation of team teaching and non-grading into the middle school. A one-year training period was devoted to developing a P.T.A. committee that could be counted upon to support the middle school objectives. Four meetings, spread throughout the year, were for the P.T.A. executive group and a P.T.A. representative from each homeroom. The group, some 60 members strong, was shown movies and slides from schools utilizing team teaching and non-grading. Discussions were held based on the information observed, and questions were promptly answered. Members of the executive committee visited schools.

During the course of the training, the P.T.A. nucleus generated a list of questions which they felt would be of common interest to other parents concerning the middle school concept. The questions included:

1. How does the elimination of the class grade structure affect the performance of the individual student?
2. What attributes of the non-graded school make it superior to the graded school structure?
3. What problems can be anticipated when a child enters a school employing the middle school concept from a conventional graded school, and likewise, what problems are anticipated when a child leaves a school employing the middle school concept and returns to the graded school?
4. What are the inherent strong and weak points in the middle school concept?
5. What unique provisions must middle school have to make team teaching effective?

Six weeks before the opening of the school, letters announcing a meeting were received by parents whose children would enroll in middle school in September. The purpose of the meeting, which was sponsored by the P.T.A., was defined as being primarily to answer enclosed questions about the middle school objective to be further implemented at the middle school. Data sheets containing information pertinent to the questions were distributed by the committee as parents entered the meeting place. The information explained the nature of the committee's experience during the past year, and how the questions had been formulated. Questions were answered by middle school professional staff members. The purpose of the meeting was fully achieved.

Two weeks before the beginning of the school year, those members of the professional staff involved in implementing the middle school objectives completed their analysis of the records of students likely to enroll in middle school. An initial group was selected to participate—it was decided that the problem of attempting to bring all middle school students into the program at once would overtax the capacity of the staff. Letters were sent to notify parents of the selection of their child to participate in the program, and to request that they agree or disagree with the proposed selection. The decision of the parents was accepted.

The professional staff at Eden Heights middle school had many problems during that first year of implementing the middle school objectives, but it was agreed that the task had been made easier by the careful attention given to the factor of *people* involved before actual implementation was initiated.

Student Programming

Innovative practices need to be included in student programming. The use of a flow network has been found useful in planning and implementing programs for the middle school. There is no intent to allege that middle school is the only school where this technique can be employed.

The particular emphasis on programming is that of including the student in the activities. The teaching teams and the student are co-architects of the student's program. As staff member plans the program with the student, they participate together in the learning situation in a student-guide relationship, and they jointly evaluate progress and then re-program. As the program is planned, the student is not restricted to a traditional lock step—that algebra may be studied only in his last year in middle school; rather the student may begin his study of algebra at any point where he and the team determine he is ready.

The professional staff will not always find traditional and formal courses of study and guides of much value. Rather they will find that developing materials to fit the particular student is the most valuable way of assisting with his continuous learning program.

Included on each teaching team will be staff members for each of the different disciplines. With the expert knowledge of each of the members, they will function cooperatively in the programming process. The recommended staff organization for a middle school is shown in Figure 4-1. A detailed description of the staff was provided in Chapter 3.

Among the purposes which the logic breakdown chart serves are (a) causes the discipline expert to break down his area into logical discussions, sub-divisions, elements, sub-elements, etc. down to the *nth* information or skill level requisite to initial discipline activity, (b) causes the discipline expert to become aware of the necessity for being able to support learning activities from the *nth* level upward to the highest event level that a particular middle schooler may be capable of reaching, (c) makes it possible for any middle schooler to begin work in a discipline at a level where progress is possible and (d) makes possible student-teacher programming in a discipline since the point at which the student is capable of selecting obtainable objectives and the point at which the expert can furnish sufficient learning support to insure those learning objectives can be ascertained.

Having developed a logic breakdown chart, the team professional is ready to construct flow networks with his students. The flow network provides a means for tying events

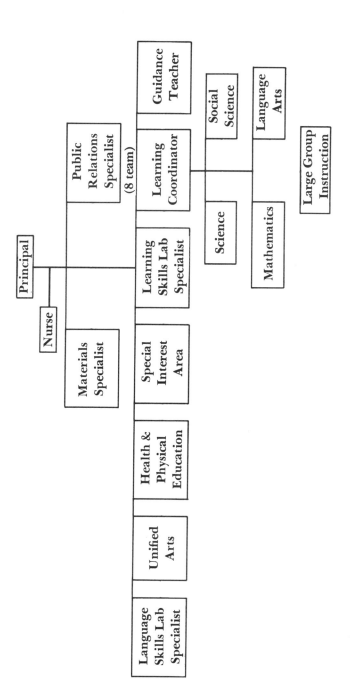

Figure 4-1 *Middle school staff organization chart.*

89

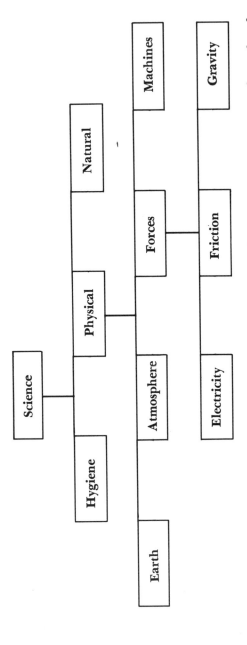

Figure 4-2 *Science logic breakdown chart.*

Application of flow networks to student programming. Flow networks are constructed and employed as described herein. The teaching team professionals begin by developing logic breakdown charts to the nth level (by the nth level we have reference to the lowest level required for a particular entering middle schooler to engage in learning activities for that given discipline.) To clarify the process for the reader, an example of a science logic breakdown chart to the fourth level is provided in figure 4-2. The nth level for a particular student could well be several unknown levels of event below the fourth.

together in time sequence order. An example from science is provided to introduce the reader to the use of the flow network in programming.

Suppose it has been determined by the professional that the student is capable of working at the 4th event level in Figure 4-2. If the student and professional agree that the student acquire an understanding of direct current electricity, the following simplified series of events would require completing in order for the objectives relative to electricity to be accomplished:

1. Learning about batteries completed
2. Learning about resistance completed
3. Learning about circuits completed
4. Learning about motors completed
5. Learning about radio completed

The events are placed in a network with the events that require learning in sequence indicated in a series path and those which may be completed simultaneously in parallel paths. The flow network of our illustration appears as shown in Figure 4-3.

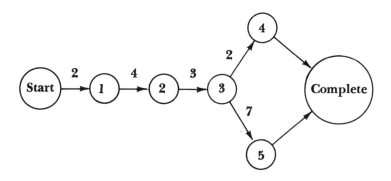

Figure 4-3 *Flow network—direct current electricity.*

The number in the circle refers to the completed events identified above. The arrows between the circles indicate activities that are undertaken in order to complete the event. The estimated times and the actual times may be included in the diagram by placing the estimated time above the arrow and the actual time below. In our example it is estimated that it will take 2 weeks to complete the activities in connection with event number one. The estimated time to complete the whole network is 16 weeks. Flow networks may be developed for any and all levels of a logic breakdown chart. Figure 4-4 shows the complexity involved as higher levels are included. A complete network for a total discipline includes all activities and events. Programming through the use of complicated networks becomes difficult when over 100 events and activities are included if the work is done entirely by hand. However, the task becomes easier when a digital program is available. Use of the computer makes tracking of student progress in a network fast and effortless. Computer printouts are available to reflect an infinite number of relationships pertinent to student activity. The flow network is consequently an invaluable tool for student programming in middle school.

Student Scheduling

Scheduling involves time. When schedules are constructed, time is the independent variable. Events and activities plotted against time are the dependent variables. All persons are influenced by schedules. A typical school calendar shows events and activities that are fixed with respect to time.

How efficient is the calendar from the individual staff member's point of view? Do vacations occur at a time which will enable the staff member to maximize his vacation hours? Are workshops and conferences held when they prove most useful? If the answers to the questions are no, then valuable resources—human resources—are being wasted.

The school calendar topic was raised to initiate thinking along this particular line. Scheduling is defined as the order-

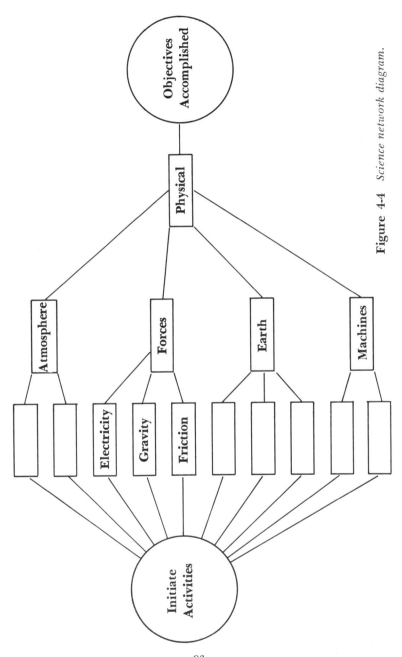

Figure 4-4 *Science network diagram.*

ing of school resources to support students in learning situations. This connotation of scheduling may be new to you. School scheduling has a tendency to be accomplished in the school calendar fashion. The criterion for middle school scheduling is the efficiency of resources used in the learning situation. Resource efficiency may be described as the use of resources in such a manner that all students are being supported in learning situations to such an extent that further assistance in the learning situation can only be provided by increasing the resources available to the school. School resources are buildings, grounds, facilities, personnel and money.

At middle school, resources are supplied to the learning situation as required. If there are 800 students in a middle school, at a given point in time, 800 unique schedules will exist. Schedules are but working tools to assist the learner and the staff in bringing order into the learning environment. The schedule guides the student in allocating time among activities and enables the staff to accomplish scheduling objectives.

The schedule is but a tool. When a tool is improperly selected to accomplish a job, the worker has no hesitancy in selecting another which is better designed to do the task. So it is with student schedules. The student schedule is formulated by the staff and the student, after review of the student's progress on his learning network. Assumptions were made that the schedule contained the optimum activities to be undertaken at the given time. The staff's level of confidence in its assumptions increases as greater understandings are obtained about the students early in their middle school years. A neophyte at Eden Heights recorded 17 schedule changes within a single school year.

The statement was made that if there were 800 students in middle school, at any given point in time, there would be 800 different schedules. Since the student population is divided among several teams, a teaching team is not assigned more than 90-100 students. The number of individual schedules for the teaching team is of a manageable size.

Scheduling of resources to meet student requirements is accomplished through daily team meetings. The length of the meeting is a function of teaching team experience and student capabilities. Usual team meetings take one to two and one-half hours. Meetings consider common matters of concern such as providing mutual teacher assistance, the operating of large group classes and laboratory use as well as evaluating individual student progress and planning for future adjustments to the student's schedule. The progress rate of several students is reviewed daily. The team tries to review every assigned student at least twice during a four-week period.

The teacher's daily schedule in middle school reflects the application of resources to learning situations as required. Time must be provided in the schedule for activities ranging from those tutorial in nature to the instruction of large groups. Whatever the nature of the activity, it is being conducted at the given time because of the need of the students for teacher support. The activity performed is the one that maximizes the use of teacher and time. An Eden Heights language art teacher's schedule is presented for a particular day. The teacher is a member of teaching team Y. The particular day was a point in time 16 months distant from the time that 90 students arrived at middle school from several surrounding neighborhood elementary schools. You are invited to compare the daily schedule shown with schedules of junior high school language arts teachers whom you know. The difference of the middle school scheduling concept will be brought home vividly to you.

A Language Arts Teacher Schedule

8:00   Work with three students who are writing a play.
8:40- 9:00 Work with 5 students initiating topics of American Folklore.

9:00- 9:30 Moderate small group discussion considering the difference between the folk tale and literary versions of tales by Irving, Twain and Sandburg—12 students.

9:30- 9:45 Work with a student who has written a legend about a famous American hero of modern times, intended to be read in the year 2100.

9:45-10:00 Work with 5 youngsters who are having trouble communicating through written work.

10:00-11:00 Teaching Team Planning Meeting.

11:00-11:30 Lunch.

11:30-12:00 Serve as discussion leader for a group of 25 students who are reviewing a novel from the standpoint of theme, character, plot and setting.

12:00-12:30 Participate in discussion with four students who have read Esther Forbes' biography, *Paul Revere and the World He Lived In.*

12:30- 1:15 Meet with Social Studies teacher and a group of 35 students and serve as group assistant to the social studies teacher.

1:15- 2:00 Work with 10 students who are having trouble researching a topic.

2:00- 3:10 Planning period (Maybe!)

3:10- 3:30 Meet with a student for individualized reading.

SELECTED READINGS

Association for Supervision and Curriculum Development. *New Insights and the Curriculum.* Washington, D.C.: National Education Association, 1963.

Bair, Medill and Richard G. Woodward. *Team Teaching in Action.* Boston: Houghton Mifflin Company, 1964.

Beggs, David W., III. "A Success Story of Small and Large Group Instruction: The Decatur-Lakeview Plan." *Overview,* 3:12; December, 1962.

Dean, Stuart E. *Elementary School Administration and Organization: A National Survey of Practices and Policies,* Bulletin No. 11. Washington, D.C.: U. S. Department of Health, Education and Welfare, Office of Education, 1960.

_____ "Teach Teaching: A Review." *School Life,* 44:5-8; September, 1961.

Devita, Joseph C. "No Homework . . . No Report Card Grades . . . Ungraded." *National Association of Secondary School Principals Bulletin,* 45:180-184; October, 1961.

Drummond, Harold D. "Team Teaching: An Assessment." *Educational Leadership* 19:160-165; December, 1961.

Ench, Jeri. "Why Not Year-Around Schools." *Saturday Review,* 82-84; September, 1966.

Fischler, Abraham S. *Modern Junior High School Science, A Recommended Sequence of Courses.* New York: Bureau of Publications, Teachers College, Columbia University, 1961.

Flanders, Ned. *et al.* "Measuring Dependence Proneness in the Classroom," *Educational and Psychological Measurement,* 21: 575-587; Autumn, 1961.

Fleming, Robert S., ed. *Curriculum for Today's Boys and Girls.* Columbus, Ohio: Charles E. Merrill Books, Inc., 1963.

Frazier, Alexander, ed. *New Insights and the Curriculum.* Washington, D.C.: Association for Supervision and Curriculum Development, 1963.

_____ "Needed: A New Vocabulary for Individual Differences." *Elementary School Journal,* 61:260-68; February, 1961.

Frymier, Jack R. "A Study of Students' Motivation to Do Good

Work in School," *Journal of Educational Research* 57:239-44; January, 1964.

Gladis, Michael. "Grade Differences in Transfer as a Function of the Time Interval Between Learning Tasks," *Journal of Educational Psychology,* 51:191-194; August, 1960.

Gladstein, Gerald A. "A New Approach for Identifying Appropriate Individual Study Behavior." *The School Review,* 71:158-169; Summer, 1963.

Griffin, William M. "The Wayland, Massachusetts, High School Program for Individual Differences." *National Association of Secondary School Principals Bulletin,* 47:118-127; March, 1963.

Henry, N. B., ed. *Individualizing Instruction.* Sixty-first Yearbook of the National Society for the Study of Education, Part I. Chicago: University of Chicago Press, 1962.

Huffmire, Donald W. "Analysis of Independent Study Projects." *Science Teacher,* 29:31-39; April, 1963.

Larmee, Roy A. and Robert Ohm. "University of Chicago Lab School Freshman Project Involves Team Teaching. New Faculty Position, and Regrouping of Students." *National Association of Secondary School Principals Bulletin,* 44:275-289; January, 1960.

Leuba, Clarence. "Using Groups in Independent Study." *Improving College and University Teaching,* 12:26-30; Winter, 1964.

Marsh, R. "Team Teaching: New Concept," *Clearing House,* 35:496-499; April, 1961.

Parker, J. Cecil, T. B. Edwards and W. H. Stegeman. *Curriculum in America.* New York: Thomas Y. Crowell Company, 1962.

Shaplin, Judson T. and Henry F. Olds, Jr., eds. *Team Teaching.* New York: Harper and Row, Publishers, 1964.

Shideler, Ernest H. "An Individualization Program." *Journal of Higher Education,* 5:91-98; February, 1934.

Shumsky, Abraham. *Creative Teaching in the Elementary School.* New York: Appleton-Century-Crofts, 1965.

Smith, Barbara. *How to Teach Junior High.* Philadelphia: The Westminster Press, 1965.

Smith, B. Othaniel and Robert H. Ennis, eds. *Language and Concepts.* Chicago: Rand McNally Company, 1961.

Taba, Hilda. *Curriculum Development: Theory and Practice.* New York: Harcourt, Brace & World, Inc., 1962.

Taylor, Calvin W. and Frank Barron (eds.) *Scientific Creativity: Its Recognition and Development.* New York: John Wiley & Sons, Inc., 1963.

Taylor, Calvin W. and Frank Barron, eds. *Scientific Creativity:*

Tewksbury, John. *Non-Grading in the Elementary School.* Columbus, Ohio: Charles E. Merrill Books, Inc., 1966.

Varner, Glenn F. "Team Teaching in Johnson H.S., St. Paul, Minn." *National Association of Secondary School Principals Bulletin,* 46:161-166; January, 1962.

Wiles, Kimball. *The Changing Curriculum of the American High School.* Englewood Cliffs, New Jersey: Prentice-Hall, Inc. 1963.

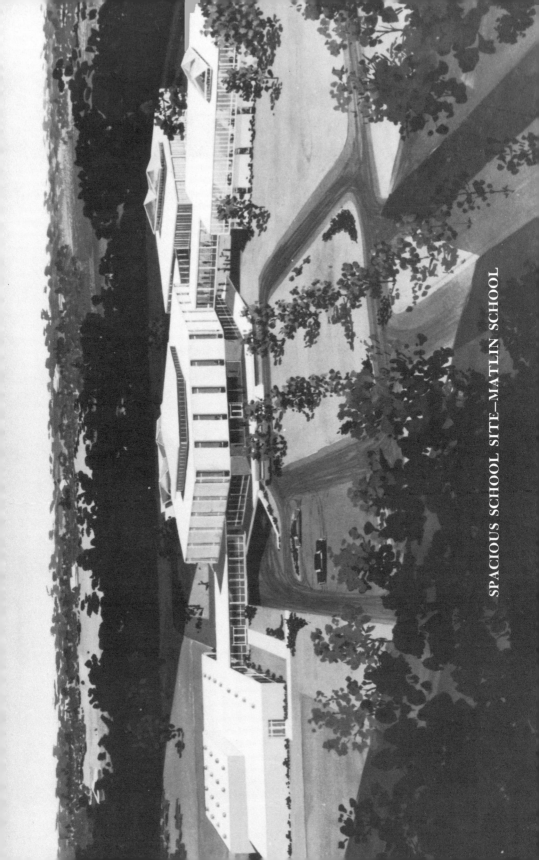

SPACIOUS SCHOOL SITE—MATLIN SCHOOL

5

Middle School Educational Plant

The Multipurpose School Plant

When planning for an educational plant, the planners must understand that a commitment is being made for today—10 years from today—and far into the future. Plants tend to become monuments to their conceivers' shortsightedness when viewed with the perspective of 20/20 hindsight thirty years later. Long term forces and factors as well as short term ones must be considered.

A strong force in the educational environment of the 1920's was the high school movement. An important factor in the movement was the college preparatory curriculum. The consequence was buildings constructed with box-like classrooms. The rooms were equipped with chalk boards and desks with a flag staff and maps being the only other furnishings. High schools have outgrown the single curriculum. School buildings constructed in the 1920's no longer are adequate.

Boards of education faced both with escalating high school enrollments and plant acquisitions costs resort to the construction of new high school buildings and to the conversion of existing high school buildings into housing for middle schoolers. The "new" middle schools are obsolete before their doors are opened to receive their first team of students. Avoidance of plant acquisition mistakes cannot be entirely prevented. Foresight becomes rather fogged when the forecast extends beyond five years.

Educational innovation is moving forward on many fronts: nongrading, variable grouping, independent study procedures, new staff utilization plans, and curricula organized for continuous student progress. The Institute for Development of Educational Activities (I.D.E.A.) of the Kettering Foundation is encouraging systematic evaluation of innovation through support to schools where innovation is presently exercised. Planning must provide a school plant capable of utilizing those innovations which improve efficiency in the learning situation.

Planning must consider the trend toward greater community use of the school plant. Research shows that communities are making increasing use of the plant on both a daily and yearly basis. The Elementary and Secondary Education Act of 1966 contains a provision for the use of health, remedial and like services by all children in the community regardless of whether they attend public or private schools.

The School Plant Planners

The planning for the proposed new or converted school plant for middle school is, as in most cases, accomplished by a team. Preferably, the team is composed of group representatives and individuals from organizations that will participate in developmental activities from design conception through plant operation. The team approach is essential if maximum benefits are to be obtained from the plant for the resources expended. Team membership will normally include school board member(s), the superintendent of schools, teachers, citizen group representative(s), educational consultant(s), and the architect. Detailed planning by the team is highly recommended before the plant design is released to an architectural engineering firm for construction. Engineering drawing changes are roughly one percent as costly to implement as brick and mortar changes. Construction changes can be implemented without affecting planned plant completion dates.

Bedford Public Schools took a unique team approach toward conceptualization of the form of middle school and the requisite plant design. Dr. Charles O. Richter, then superintendent, planned for a middle school conference to determine to what degree current planning could achieve an education program and a building that will adequately prepare the students for the future. The conference, jointly sponsored by the Bedford Public Schools, Mount Kisco, New York, and the Educational Facilities Laboratory (E.F.L.), was attended by seventeen persons representing fifteen separate areas including psychology, teaching, architecture, industrial design, city planning, programmed learning, library science, school administration, teacher training and public policy. Findings of the conference were summarized in a report by the E.F.L. staff and presented to the Bedford Board of Education, and through the board, to the citizens of the community. Few school systems have emulated Bedford's conceptual phase of middle school development. Fox Lane middle school enrolled student teams for the first time during the summer of 1966.

Teachers

Teachers pose a problem in school plant planning. The new middle school plant must contain facilities to enable the teaching teams to offer the required support in learning situations. The middle school concept of change demands innovation and the spirit of inquisitiveness to devise evaluation procedures for testing innovation effectiveness. Among current middle school innovations are team teaching, non-grading and independent study. Teaching staffs in school systems which feature self-contained classrooms in the elementary school and departmentalized instruction in the junior high school are not being challenged to implement innovations. When these teachers learn that a new middle school is to be opened and they are asked to participate in planning for the school with an opening date only several months hence, are we being fair to the teachers? What valid contributions can teachers make to middle school plant planning under the related circumstances?

You probably have seen the cartoon of the MAD magazine character with such epithets under it as "Six months ago I couldn't even spell engineer and now I is one"; the analogy applies here. Teaching staffs are being asked to undertake planning responsibilities for which they haven't the necessary background. Often, they are sent on trips to see a middle school in operation or are given suggested reading lists to prepare them for plant planning activity only weeks before important architectural inputs are required.

Teachers must be an integral part of plant planning teams. However, when a school district must staff a new middle school with existing teaching resources, an effort must be made to train the teachers about the middle school and its instructional innovations. Since the teachers or their representatives will participate in plant planning, familiarization is necessary regarding equipment and furnishing currently available. Training must be well developed before teachers are brought into discussions with an architect and engineer intending to firm up the middle school plant design prior to engineering drawing release.

School Architect

To be an effective member of the plant planning team, the architect must understand middle school philosophy. He must appreciate the significant differences evidenced in the local hue that will guide educational programs planning in the proposed school plant. He must appreciate trends in education so that his plant design of today has the flexibility to meet tomorrow's requirements.

The architect team member must understand that he is a member of the planning team. He *is not* the team. He has many avenues open to him to gain better understandings of how middle school philosophy impinges upon design and construction. Numerous middle schools plants are available for visitation and inspection. Among middle schools that have been constructed since 1960 are those at Amory, Mississippi; Barrington, Illinois; Centerville, Ohio; Mount Kisco, New York and Saginaw, Michigan.

The architect furnishes the analytical capability to the team. He makes studies to evaluate ideas generated by the team and furnishes feedback showing the impact of design conceptualization in terms of cost, schedule and plant performance. He builds computer programs to simulate the operation of suggested plant designs and enables their relative efficiencies to be determined. He builds scale models of particular plant facilities to enable interface requirements between facilities to be determined. He conducts studies involving materials, floor covering, lighting, heating and the like. He provides the engineering services to the team not available anywhere else.

The possibility of continuing the planning team's existence into the operational phase is becoming a necessity. Innovation is the life blood of the middle school. Many middle schools, whose mortar has barely cured, are identifying construction change requirements. The Bedford middle school conference recognized that a new plant would require periodic rearranging. It was suggested that the architect be kept on a retainer to participate in periodic reviews of plant performance and to assist in planning changes needed to keep pace with changing programs.

Administration

The Administration is responsible for school plant planning. It may delegate some of those responsibilities to a planning team. The planning team does not then become totally responsible for the plant acquisition. The team is responsible only for the duties delegated. The administration is accountable to the school board and to the community for the school plant acquired.

Experience tells us that when school plants are planned solely from the top down, the plant's potential is not fully utilized. A staff not properly trained or persuaded about the merits of new program will continue old practices in the new environment. The administration must insure that its professional staff understands and is persuaded to try new learning innovations essential to middle school operation.

The administration need not accept all team plant recommendations. Rejected recommendations need to be discussed with team members. When the team learns the reasons for rejection, they are less likely to feel that their work is being casually thrown aside. Rejection without explanations adversely affects future team contributions and serves as the basis for dissatisfaction with the new plant at a later date.

The administration signs off on the final architect and engineer design. It must guard against personal bias in the process. A principal in a Florida county, which was planning for a new middle school, lacked faith in the staff's ability to cope with extensive team teaching and flexible scheduling. A plant was built with all self-contained classrooms. The administration was subsequently replaced by one which had a background in nongraded programming. Now lack of flexibility is regretted in the new plant.

Site Selection

Is there an ideal site for the middle school? The question is a moot one. Rather than seeking an ideal site, middle school plant planners must try to determine optimum sites for the given school district. The determination of the optimum site must be based upon the ideal site criterion and a set of factors over which the planners may have little or no control: for example, bonded indebtedness limitations, availability of land, presence of school buildings that are part of the local heritage, attitudes of parents toward transporting students and the availability of general services at prospective sites away from congested areas.

The ideal criterion grows from the nature of the middle school and from the community that it is intended to serve. The middle school is the school of change, innovation, discovery and inquiry. It is a place to develop skills and capabilities. It is a place of activity, a place for reflection, a place for study and a place for self-realization. The site criterion must reflect these attributes.

Middle schools must serve the adult community as well as middle schoolers. Many middle school facilities are suitable for adult use such as auditoriums, cafeterias, health centers and unified arts areas. The criterion must reflect such facility use on a non-interference basis.

The ideal criterion for a middle school site encompasses:

Aesthetically pleasing surroundings

An environment that can serve as an outdoor laboratory

A location that is close to feeder schools

Ample land for present plant needs and adequate for surrounding park-like area

Central location that is readily accessible to adults in the community

Sufficient land to provide for the inclusion of one or more middle schools when required or to provide for conversion to another type educational facilities at some future date

Natural geographic features that separate the site from surrounding areas to insure the site from being surrounded by construction at future times.

An area that has a long-term useful life ahead

An area that affords integration experience for the middle school population.

Facilities

The middle school may have two types of space requirements—space occupied by activities participated in by the total school population and space occupied by student team activity. An architectural design practice for campus type middle school plants is to locate the space for common activities in one building and to provide space for two or more teams in separate buildings situated around the common activity building as shown in Figure 5-1.

Buildings providing space for team activities are identified as houses. Provisions for separate space allocation may be accomplished in conventionally designed buildings through assignment of wings to team activity.

Team housing. An important aspect of facility design for team housing is flexibility. Flexibility is defined as the characteristic that enables a facility to be readily adapted to team teaching staff capabilities and to the learning situation requirements. Flexibility places a demand upon the facility designer to conceive an educational laboratory. The education laboratory is envisioned as a facility with a large internal area free from fixed wall obstructions. It requires a floor structure that permits the installation of portable/movable partitions whenever deemed necessary by the staff. It necessitates the installation of lighting, acoustical materials and heating and ventilation in a manner which makes all parts of the area equally susceptible to rearrangement. The educational laboratory is a permissive environment which by itself does not place limitations upon the staff toward innovations and change.

Given an educational laboratory, you are challenged to consider how you would initially arrange the space for the student/professional staff team to maximize area utilization. The student team is composed of 10 to 14-year-olds. The solution evolved by one school planning group for an open area is shown in Figure 5-3. The layout suggests that the teaching team supporting student learning has not moved far into middle school innovation. The layout provides only for medium and small groups and for planning centers. Movement through a wing arranged as in B figure can be a problem since fixed corridors no longer exist. It is sug-

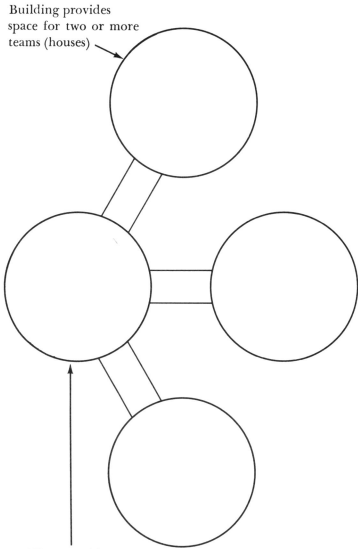

Building provides
space for two or more
teams (houses)

Building provides space
for common activities

Figure 5-1 *Plan view of campus type middle school plant.*

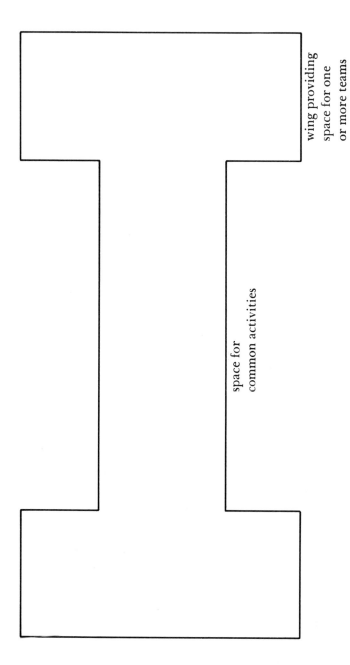

Figure 5-2 *Plan view of a middle school.*

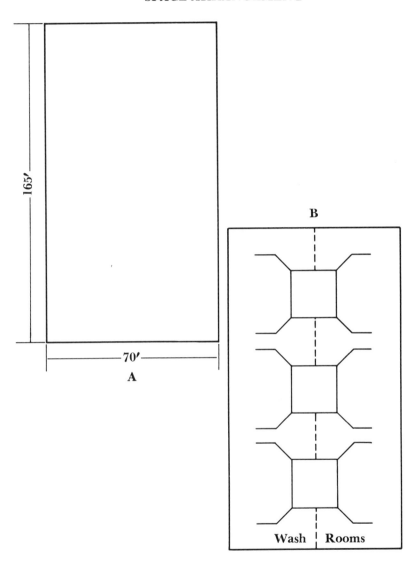

Figure 5-3 *Partitions arranged for medium size group area. Solid lines represent demountable walls; dotted lines represent folding partitions that can produce small group areas. Squares in this diagram represent teacher's planning center.*

111

gested that visual or acoustical schemes be devised as possible solutions to the travel problem.

A particular teaching team area contains a unique arrangement of equipment, partitions and furniture ordered by the professional operating there. The features to be incorporated are delineated by the middle school. The features include student centers, spaces for independent study, small and large group centers, science laboratories and learning centers. The student center affords a place for students and staff to meet informally. It serves as a supplemental study area and social center. The student center shown is achieved with a simple arrangement of partitions and furniture.

Space for groups of various sizes is required. Large group centers are built up as needed. Careful planning is required to determine space and equipment requirements. Equipment available to a large group center must include portable chalk boards, tack boards, electronic reception center and demonstration materials. The physical existence of the large group center is a function of teaching team planning. Resources are put to other uses upon the center's demise.

Small group areas require facility space for longer time periods. Space must be provided for 5 to 12 students. Less time is necessary for area preparation. Requirement for equipment is austere. Significant materials include chalk board, easels, and screens. Ancillary equipment is supplied as the situation demands.

The science laboratory contains the only fixed equipment in the teaching team areas. The indoor science laboratory is an extension of the outdoor laboratory and reflects the association through provisions for natural and physical science study. The laboratory is intended to foster inquiry and experimentation. Ample laboratory working space is required so that equipment needing to remain assembled for several days can remain undisturbed. Each student must have an equipment storage place of his own. The laboratory requires areas for demonstration and equipment storage and serves as a museum of classical student projects.

LIBRARY-MATERIALS CENTER

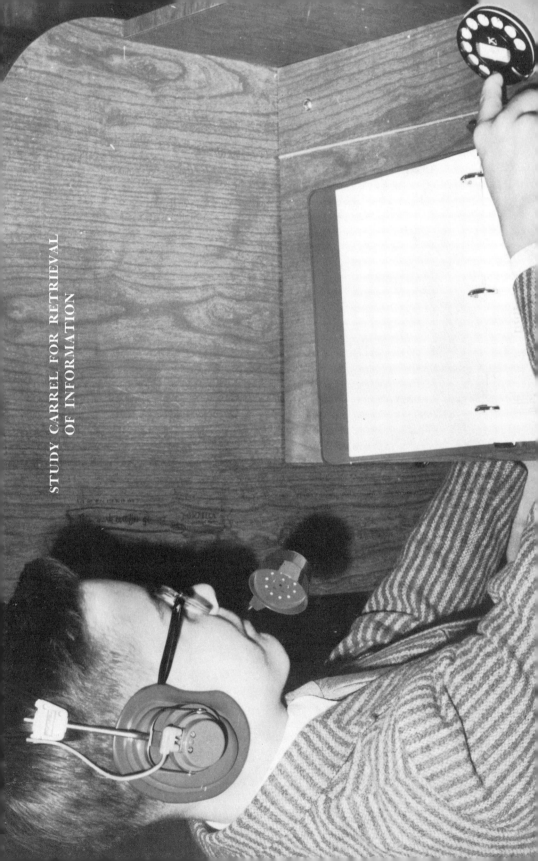

STUDY CARREL FOR RETRIEVAL OF INFORMATION

Middle school students participating in independent study activities must rely upon a number of media to assist them. Since much study can be more efficiently accomplished from the team area than from the library/materials center, a means for making library resources in the team area is necessary. A partial solution to the problem is the dial select system whereby students can dial the library/materials center for playback of tapes and recordings. Some carrels (wet) are provided with the equipment for selecting desired audio-visual materials and reception of transmitted materials. A typical wet type carrel is shown. Approximately one-fourth of the quantity of carrels provided for middle school should be of the wet type.

Carrels are provided for use as independent work stations. They are placed strategically throughout the area. The recommended carrel type seats four students. Partitions extending above the horizontal working surface are retractable, thereby making conversion of the carrel into a flat type table easily accomplished. Portions are covered with sound absorbent materials to reduce noise interference among students using a common carrel. Materials not in use by the student may be stored below the working surface in a rack provided. The recommended carrel type is shown in an accompanying photograph.

At least one house in the school should provide a "space" laboratory center. The facility as a minimum requires a photographic dark room, telescope and planetarium. A planetarium of the type shown in the photograph can be of great value to the students.

Unified arts center. A unified arts center is designed to permit students to discover their capabilities and develop new skills. The center enables students to make choices as to the media they desire to use and the skill they wish to improve. The openness of the area makes readily available several craft regions so that a variety of projects may be completed. The use of portable equipment makes large and small group work in the region feasible. Equipment is

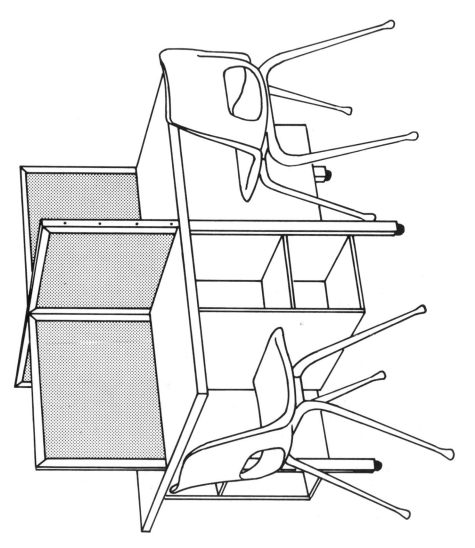

STUDY CARREL

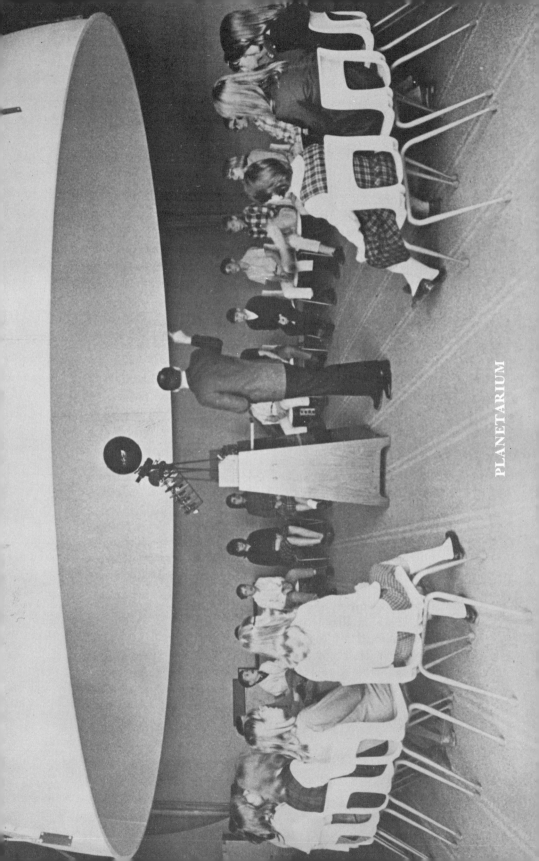

PLANETARIUM

permanently installed only in cases where performance and safety requirements dictate. Independent work areas are made available for project work through the use of portable partitions.

Music center. An important criterion for the music center is spaciousness. Vocal and instrumental areas both need large spaces permanently enclosed and designed to be non-echoic. Portable equipment and walls within the large space provide flexibility for large and small groups. Studios are available to individual students or small groups for practice or listening. The housing of music, records, tapes and instruments are conveniently located and readily accessible for students working independently or in groups. There is freedom to be creative, to develop talents and to enjoy the work of great composers in this aesthetically pleasing area. This area provides for the portable electronic reception center. Having the music center located near the unified arts area affords a means for combining works of many student artists.

Library-materials center. A spacious library is required with adequate lighting and a quality of openness. The accompanying library photograph illustrates these characteristics. The library serves as a repository for learning materials and as a research center for the student. Information may be easily obtained from many sources. Seminar rooms are provided where the student can review movies, filmstrips, tapes, microfilm, recordings and records. Seating arrangements utilize individual study carrels, (some equipped with television monitors), small work area spaces, and informal, comfortable furnishings for reading and study.

A most important feaure of the library/materials center is the staff. The librarian must assist the middle school student in a swift and efficient search for data. Data retrieval becomes more important as the magnitude of the center's resources increase. An electronic search/retrieval system is necessary when the volume of material to be searched for is very large.

The commons. The students at middle school need a place where they can meet informally to talk with their friends. The student teams tend to fragmentize and individualize the student body. Students are involved most of the day with individual and team activities. A time and place is needed where they may meet. The place is the Commons. The time may be any afternoon until 5:00 p.m. at the close of the afternoon formal activities.

The Commons is a large area located in a central location. It serves as the dining and food service area. The food service area is completely closed off from the remainder of the room. Normal furnishings in the dining area are tables and chairs for small groups. The use of some type of automatic food dispensing equipment is of importance to this growing group of students.

The Commons is a versatile room. It can be converted from an unencumbered dining area into rooms of various sizes depending upon requirements. Conversion to small group spaces is effected through use of portable/movable partitions. Electrical services permit use of audio-visual equipment. Modularized construction type props permit the erection of stage and backdrops for scheduled student performances. Having the Commons extend to an outside terrace has many advantages. Students and community groups use the area for dining and meetings. Ingress and egress to the Commons must be on a non-interference basis with other school activities.

Health and physical education center. Specialized facilities are required both indoors and outdoors to accommodate the health and physical education program. The program features intramural sports, games, attention to individual fitness, self-testing and small group activities. Many areas of green are needed for the outdoor program. Small groups utilize some of the areas of green for their activities. A sheltered area permits many outdoor activities to be continued outdoors under adverse weather conditions.

Indoor areas provide for many activities. Portable equipment and furnishings enable the gymnasium to be used for physical activities and as an auditorium. The indoor area must be accessible for community use without having to enter adjoining school building areas. Storage and housing of equipment calls for space to be available both for indoor and outdoor programs.

Electronic center and portable reception centers. The electronic center is the transmission station for audio and television information throughout the middle school plant. The center is capable of transmitting audio tapes, video tapes or direct broadcast from either a school plant location or an outside channel. The receiving stations for the transmissions are the portable reception centers and wet carrels located in team areas and in the library/materials center. The portable reception center has the capability for recording visual and audio activities.

Consolidation of all middle school common facilities in one building or general location of the school plant is good practice. The campus type school design makes the practice feasible. The Fox Lane Middle School in Mount Kisco houses common facilities in an octagonally shaped structure. Floor layouts for the structure are shown in the accompanying photographs.

The Fox Lane "arts" building evidences several features about common activities areas in middle school that need recognition. Requirements for the various areas will be discussed subsequently. Starting with the third level cross section photograph, it can be seen that all of the unified arts are clustered. No walls artificially compartmentalize the various areas. A student can move from a drawing table in graphics, to the metal area for making a pattern and to the wood shop for fabrication of an article without even walking through a door. A similar layout can be shown in the ceramic, art, domestic science and sewing area. Stairwell doors separate the unified arts into two general areas which, from the middle school viewpoint, is unfortunate.

The second level cross-section photograph pinpoints another middle school feature—independent study. The impression gained from looking at the picture is one of spaciousness, openness and lightness. The space provided enables the student to pursue his study in pleasant surroundings. Stacks are open to the student; rooms, for using materials requiring special equipment for viewing, and carrels, where concentrated study can be carried out, are available.

The first level cross-section photograph demonstrates still another middle school aspect, that of providing the required support in the learning situation. Sound laboratories and an audio-visual facility are provided to assist in making available those materials which the learning situation requires.

Facility design reflections. School plants represent the commitment of educational resources for both now and the future. Effective plant planning requires consideration of both short and long term educational objectives. Responsiveness is achieved through incorporating conditions for flexibility. The term is defined to mean that the school plant does not limit the support that human resources can contribute to the student learning situation by its physical characteristics.

Facilities envisioned for the middle schools have developed over the past several years. Much credit for the current middle school design can be given to the Educational Facilities Laboratory (EFL). Documents, published by EFL, reporting research and experimentation involving middle school facilities design, include discussion of educational television, modern classroom design, schools without walls, the acoustical environment of school buildings and urban renewal school problems. EFL contributes to the new look in school facilities for the 10 to 14-year-olds by sponsoring research and experimentation in the design of new school plants. The Pleasant Hills Middle School near Pittsburgh, Pennsylvania, and McIntosh Middle School in Sarasota County, Florida, are two among many schools who were EFL grant recipients.

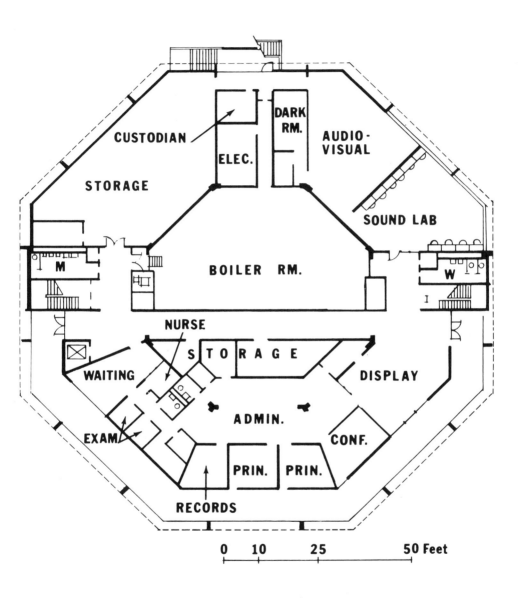

**FOX LANE COMMON FACILITY
1st FLOOR**

123

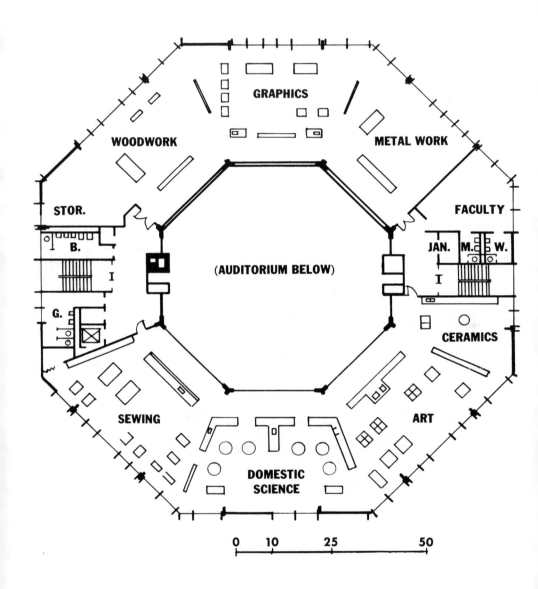

GRAPHICS

WOODWORK

METAL WORK

STOR.

FACULTY

B.

JAN. M. W.

I

I

G.

(AUDITORIUM BELOW)

CERAMICS

SEWING

ART

DOMESTIC
SCIENCE

0   10   25   50

FOX LANE COMMON FACILITY
2nd FLOOR

124

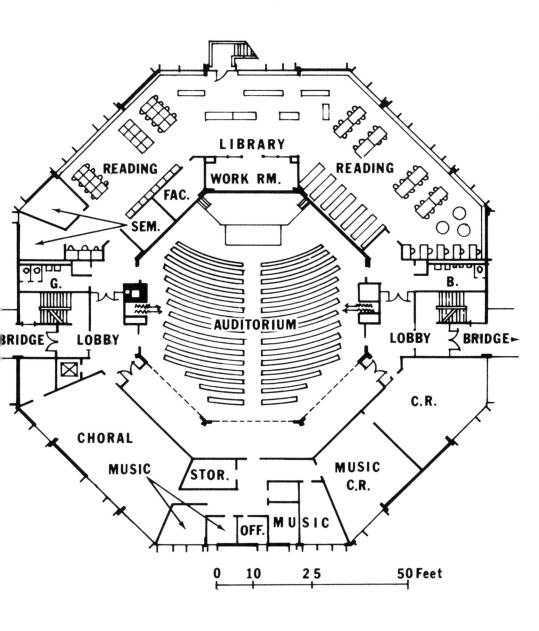

FOX LANE COMMON FACILITY
3rd FLOOR

125

SELECTED READINGS

American Association of School Administrators. *Planning American's School Buildings.* Washington, D.C.: A.A.S.A., 1960.

Beggs, David W., III and James L. Olivero. "Place Out of Space . . . The Independent Study Carrel . . . and a Variety of Studies in Lakeview H.S., Decatur, Illinois." *National Association of Secondary School Principals Bulletin,* 46:192-202; January, 1962.

Chase, Dave. "The School Library as an Instructional Materials Center." *Peabody Journal of Education,* 41:15-18; September, 1963.

Clinchy, Evans. *Profiles of Significant Schools—Two Middle Schools, Saginaw Township, Michigan.* New York: Educational Facilities Laboratories, Inc., 1960.

Conant, James B. *The Education of American Teachers.* New York: McGraw-Hill Book Company, 1963.

Educational Facilities Laboratories, Inc. *Profiles of Significant Schools—Schools Without Walls.* New York: Educational Facilities Laboratories, Inc. 1965.

Ellsworth, R. E. and H. D. Wagener. *The School Library—Facilities for Independent Study in the Secondary School.* New York: Educational Facilities Laboratories, Inc., 1963.

Evans, B. F. "Genealogy of the House Plan," *Educational Executive Overview,* 3:31-33; November, 1962.

Giaudrone, A. and H. R. Snodgrass. "School-Within-A-School Offers Pleasant Uncrowded Learning Atmosphere," *The Nation's Schools,* 69:58-62; June, 1962.

Gores, Harold B. "What Principals Should Know About New Developments in School Design," *National Association of Secondary School Principals Bulletin,* 47:190-200; April, 1963.

Krohn, Mildred L. "Learning and the Learning Center," *Educational Leadership,* 21:217-222; January, 1964.

Shaw, Archibald B., *et al.* "Space for Individual Learning." *Overview,* 4:30-40; March, 1963.

Thelen, Herbert A. *Education and the Human Quest.* New York: Harper & Row, Publishers, 1960.

6

Middle School
of the
Future

Harbingers of Change

The middle school is the school of change and innovation. It is the school responsible for providing learning support to the middle schoolers during the change period of their lives. To do an even more effective job of providing that support, the middle school must constantly review and evaluate its program. It must be ever on the alert to exploit those innovations that promise to contribute to the extended learning capabilities of its students. It must strive to develop new learning resources and to update the old ones. It must look at its professionals and cause those professionals to become even more visionary respecting their support of learning. It must constantly seek to improve communication links among students, parents, community and professionals. It must strive toward that unity of purpose that makes for dedication to effort by all those involved with middle school. It seeks to optimize actions that result in the achievement of self-realization and self-fulfillments of all those involved in perfecting middle school education. It must look continually at the middle school physical environment to assure that the high prized quality of flexibility is maintained. The middle school of the future cannot be the middle school of the present.

The term middle school is a generic one suggesting that it covers activities between other points. Already can be seen school organizations that encompass different age structure and program features from the ones enumerated in our concept. In the future, we are even more interested in investigating the optimum organizational patterns for schools and postulation of their effects upon student populations. The investigations might cause consternation in the minds of those looking for the security of a non-changing educational world. For now, we are going to continue to identify the school for 10 to 14-year-olds as a middle school. We believe that the referenced age group will populate the middle school of the future. Our minds are not closed to new findings relative to physical, social and psychological characteristics of children. If and when research indicates that the age limits for middle school be extended in either direction for more effective learning, then due consideration must be given to the inclusion of students other than 10 to 14-year-olds in the middle school concept developed.

Technology. Schools have been identified as the last strongholds of the hand crafts. The claim is with some justification. Some educational practices are centuries old; teachers in many instances teach like those who taught before them. As the middle ages weaver taught his apprentice son the crafts of his trade so have the skills of teaching been handed down through the ages. Thousands of years after the first schools were established, the problem of how learning occurs is as intriguing as it was then. Lack of adequate theories as to the nature of learning has contributed to the educational practices being poorly developed for achieving optimum student achievements. The lack of adequate learning theories is hindering the exploitation of electronic technology for the benefit of education. Even the existence of present uncertain situations is not going to deter ultimately the application of technology to the support of the learning situation. Technology has too much to offer in the areas of data processing, handling, storage, retrieval, and transmissions to be ignored by education. On the other hand, even if education desired to turn its back upon technology, it could not. Factors have been set in motion that promise to make industry a partner in the educational endeavor. The schools no longer have an exclusive lock upon the educational process.

Industry's interest in education has steadily increased over the last several years. The need to update its own employees in proficiency, ranging all the way from executive leadership to the soldering of electrical leads on a terminal board, has caused industry to develop an interest in establishing efficient educational methods. The continual complexity in the design of equipment necessitates the developments of various manuals for people in the field to use in the installation, maintenance and repair of the equipment. In-plant programs have to be developed to train employees of purchasers of hardware in its use and the like. The military departments buy billions of dollars of hardware annually from industry. Industry must train the initial cadres of military instructors who in turn will be the teachers for the field personnel. To accomplish the training, the military departments spend up to 10 percent of the cost of hardware for training programs, manuals of various types and complicated training equipment. From their own interest in training and with the electronic equipment, it is possible to build to assist in the functions of information, processing, storage, retreival, transmission and reduction; there is little wonder then that industry has turned to look at the educational market.

Educators long familiar with the old line book companies might not realize the association that has been occurring within recent years between industrial firms and the book makers. Figure 6-1 is a compilation showing alliances now existing among leading companies in the electronics industry, commercial sources of educational materials and mass communication companies. The alliances are the results of acquisitions, mergers and joint ventures perpetrated to give the companies involved a better posture for acquiring a share of educational sales.

Industry hopes to enter the educational market place from two aspects: hardware, which consists of the physical equipment for performing those tasks previously stated, and software. Software includes computer programs, the information data base, procedures for organizing the data base, personnel procedures and training, and evaluation procedures and materials necessary to satisfy the purchaser's requirements. Industry's interest in the educational market was heightened with the passage of the Elementary and Secondary Education Act of 1965 which provides for large federal grants to the schools for the purchase of textbooks, library books, audio visual equipment and so forth. The bill increased the Office of Education's research and development activities giving it the right to contract with both profit and non-profit organizations for the first time.

Hardware use in education has been limited in the past because of inadequate software or, more correctly, nonexisting software. The facets of software have been indicated. Among the facets, the computer program holds the fascination for education, but programs cannot be constructed until an adequate data base has been developed. The data base in education can be said to be the educational specification for the optimum education for each student attending America's public schools. Education has been based upon a set of cardinal principals established in 1918. It is suggested that new educational principles more viable to the space age would include: capacity for inquiry, problem-solving competence, skill in communications, familiarity with organized discipline, an appreciation for the arts and democratic com-

ELECTRONIC COMPANIES AND MASS COMMUNICATION COMPANIES

	CBS	Cowles	General Electric / Times Inc.	IBM	Minnesota Mining / Newsweek	Raytheon	RCA	Reader's Digest / Sylvania	Xerox
SOURCES	Creative Play-Things		Silver Burdett			Edex			University Microfilms
OF		Education Association	General Learning Corp.		Studies now in progress to publish current event materials	Dage-Bell		Studies now in progress on electronics system for education	Basic systems
EDUCATIONAL		College Publishing Corp.		Science Research Association		Macalaster Scientific Corp.			American Education Publication
						D:C Heath			
MATERIALS							Random House		

Figure 6-1 *Company alliances for furthering industry efforts in the education market place.*

mitment. These principles are included in the middle school concept. The principles themselves are not sufficient in themselves to form a data base for a computer program, but the middle school is.

The middle school places the emphasis on the individual student where it must be located for education in the space age. The school exists for the purpose of supporting the student in the learning situation. The student shares in his programming and progresses toward goals that he has had a part in selecting. The support provided is in terms of what is optimum for him. The role of the teacher is that of a counselor and guide. Independent study and small group meetings utilize the large part of the student's time. Large groups are convened only when situations exist that make such size groups the most effective and efficient vehicle for supporting the accomplishment of common learning objectives. Now a data base exists upon which to build a computer program. It is still a long way from a design baseline to full blown computer program, but without the design baseline the cause is hopeless.

Work has already been started to compile the information related to specific disciplines. Since the late 1950's, experts in selected disciplines have been trying to organize their material into more effective learning programs—programmed learning. Science has been particularly treated in this regard through the efforts of the National Science Foundation. Many new science curricula have been developed. The movement toward more systematic compiling of materials and the analysis of significant fact concepts and rules will receive increased emphasis in the near term future. The trend toward independent study is being felt at all levels from the elementary through graduate schools. Students' general dissatisfaction with the lecture method of instruction promises to cause a general revision in teaching procedures. The effect may be particularly pronounced at the college levels where students/teachers ratios tend to be low yet where the degree of impersonalness is greatest. The impersonal relationship existing between the student and his instructors can lead to elimination of the lecture method as a prime instructional method and to the possible switching of a large number of talented professionals from the classroom to the task of compiling information for computer programs.

The "how do students learn" aspect of programming is being considered by some of America's most talented educational reformers. New insights into learning promise to give clues to how material must be organized to meet the learning requirements of different age children. The work of these individuals seem to say that children at the middle school will find learning more stimulating when methods are followed that cause children to become involved in the learning situation through inquiry and discovery. Studies are underway to determine how children assimilate material into their composite learning behavior patterns and how such learnings are utilized to provide insight into new situations. The probings will go far toward supplying an understanding essential to constructing optimum learning sequences.

Somewhat of an anomaly is growing out of the studies performed. The anomaly relates to the place of knowledge in the learning situation. Traditional education has placed "go-no go" on knowledge. You either know the names of the five largest rivers and their tributaries or you don't. It's as simple as that to the lover of knowledge for knowledge's sake.

The reformers insist that the ability to use the knowledge as a tool in the learning situation is much more important than knowing the information. Information can be stored in memories of various kinds other than human so why must the emphasis be upon learning facts. The modern computers are information sponges. Even a small computer can store up to 40,000 bits of information through the use of magnetic tapes; it is possible to compile quantities of facts restricted only by the resources available to produce the tapes.

The concept that knowledge utilization supplants knowledge acquisition in the learning hierarchy of the student fits well into the framework of support available from the computer and its software. A program can be formulated and placed into a computer involving a given situation related to one or several disciplines. It is then possible to confront the student with a problem situation where many alternative tactics and strategies are available that will lead to a solution. He will be able to make decisions and, through the use of the computer, observe the effects of his decisions.

The student and the computer become a team working together to solve problems. The computer stores the information through a program designed to permit different routes to be exercised on the way toward problem solution; the student utilizes all information available to him. The effect of utilization of knowledge available is revealed as the student plays the games.

Professionals. The proponents of cooperative teaching speak loud and vocally in the 1960's. They see the demise of the self-contained classrooms by the 1980's. They believe the job of the teacher is far too complex for a single teacher to handle several disciplines. The result of the cooperative teaching drive may be seen from coast to coast in America. More and more schools are attempting to implement some type of team teaching plans. The schools tend to be modest in their approaches toward instruction innovations. The important point is that at least some steps are being taken. The detrimental side of the coin is that some of the innovations are beginning without the requisite philosophical and psychological understandings.

Those educational leaders who are in the forefront of the movement to encourage experimentation and innovation in American schools note the unreceptive attitude on the part of many school executives to change. This tendency to maintain the status quo is one of the forces resisting the middle school movement. Fortunately, the tides of change are swirling too strongly about these individuals to be any longer denied. Even in a large city in a New England state long noted for its conservative practices and obedience to authority, change is occurring. Change must and will ocur in education practices as attention becomes focused upon the changed social patterns of the city and the paucity of the current educational program. Forces working to bring the change are both educational and economic. In the suburbs of the city, models exist of what middle school education has to offer the students and the community. The suburbs have indicated a willingness to bus certain ethnic group students to the suburban schools to participate in middle school programs. When the students find out what education is like outside the large city, the demands for change will echo throughout the core city. As to the economic aspect, the city is deprived of the benefits of federal grants pending solution to some of its educational problems.

School executives are being afforded information relative to change from many quarters. Their professional journals are filled with articles thumping the need for change and innovation. The literature contains many examples of how schools are embarking upon programs aimed at improving the quality and effectiveness of education for the individual student. Nor are the professional journals the only source speaking out for change. Private foundations are taking an active part to encourage innovation and change. A leader in the private fund arena is the Charles F. Kettering Foundation's Institute for the Development of Educational Activities (IDEA). The Institute was organized for the primary purpose of stimulating the development, evaluation, and dissemination of various means for improving rationality and efficiency in American education. Four Fellows Institutes for school administrators were held by IDEA during the summer of 1966. The theme of the Institute was something of a tripod centering around creativity in education and innovations in learning tied together by the role of history and the social sciences. The school executives who fail to respond to the challenge of change and innovation in education should be carefully examined for evidence of life, for truly the spirit of adventure, inquiry, and discovery has passed from him.

Parents and community. The middle school is the educational institution of change and innovation. The middle school concept is evolving to provide learning support to students during the most rapidly changing period of their lives. It arrives on the educational scene at a time when professionals recognize that an incremental step must be taken to improve the effectiveness and efficiency of education for the 10 to 14-year-old students. Despite the recognized need for change and innovation, the likeliness of such events occurring rests in part upon the willingness of parents and the community to accept change and innovation in their schools. Boards of Education are elected officials in the United States and are responsible to the attitudes and feelings of their constituents. Quite often board members double in brass as parents and community leaders in no school-related activities. If the feelings and attitudes of parents and the community are not responsive to change and innovation, the probability of successfully introducing change and innovation into the school is low.

What is the position of parents and the community most likely to be between the present time period and the post 1975 era relative to change and innovation in the nation's schools? A lead to parental and community feelings and attitudes toward such change is supplied through a study conducted by Gallup International, Incorporated, for the Charles F. Kettering Foundation in 1966. The findings show that parents and community are more ready to accept change and innovation than professional educators are. Among the innovations that are accepted by the people are teaching students how to organize their work and their thinking, how to concentrate and how to analyze problems; use of the school as community and adult learning centers; team teaching; special vocational training tied into industry; nongraded schools, or placement based upon level of achievement; independent study—plan for spending at least 40 percent of a student's time in independent study; and programmed instruction. While many persons may not fully understand what the change and innovations entail, tacit approval to proceed with these concepts essential to the middle school is seen. School officials in Chicago, Detroit, and Philadelphia have discovered an enthusiastic response to programs informing parents about program innovations.

A Look at the New School

Considering the nature of future middle schools is exciting. The future holds implications for those of us who are now serving as educational professionals as well as for those persons who will join the profession in the coming years. The future is uncertain; technological, economic, political and social changes differing from those contemplated may enter the situation between the present and the future and significantly alter forecasted conditions. Even so, forecasts must be made to enable planners to establish tentative programs.

Forecasts can be made in a systematic fashion. TEMPO, a scientific research unit which has conducted studies for such clients as the Universities of California, Chicago, and Michigan, and for General Motors and General Electric has formulated guidelines to forecasting. The guidelines are (a) estimate the future environment in human, scientific, political and social terms, (b) put together possible new concepts and product designs in response to business prospects as seen in (a) and (c), and test new concepts against available resources and potential benefits. We explored guideline (a) in the first section of the present chapter. Postulated middle school programs are conceived in relation to technology, professions and parents/community considerations provided in (a).

Futura Middle School. Team teaching, nongrading, independent study and small group sessions have lived through the 1960's and are ensconced at Futura in the late 1970's. The innovations of the sixties are the modus operandi of the 1970's. The seventies witness an innovation in the teaching team composition. Teaching teams in the sixties usually consisted of a learning coordinator, teachers in the science, social science, language arts, and mathematics disciplines, and a teacher counselor. The Futura teaching team has eight members and a teacher counselor for the same size student team (90 to 100 students) as the sixties had. The team teaching change occurring affects the social science discipline. The former single team member is replaced by four persons and the discipline is recorded as decision analysis. The decision analysis teaching team members are experts in the social science areas of psychology, anthropology, economics and education. Decision makers have found that decision-making is not nicely compartmentalized into mathematics, science, or language arts to the exclusion of other disciplines, but that decision-making crosses the lines of many subject areas. The assignment of all social scientists at Futura to decision analysis doesn't mean that decision analysis in the middle school is restricted only to the social science discipline. The social scientists use the services of other team members in the decision analysis area as required.

The nucleus of the decision analysis discipline at Futura is the simulated exercise. The use of the simulated exercise enables the students to make decisions and to observe the consequences of their decision-making actions. Decisions do not tend to be right or wrong, but rather some decisions lead to more desirable consequences. The simulated exercises alert the students to the difference between drawing rational decisions based upon available information and seat of the pants judgments based on nothing more than firm intuition or hunches.

The hub of the simulated exercise is the scenario. Scenarios may be purchased from the educational product makers, but the teaching team at Futura prefers to construct its own. The more talented students at middle school undertake projects to develop new exercises in areas of special interest. Maintaining the usefulness of scenarios for several successive groups of students tends to be a challenge to student integrity. Student participation in the simulation may determine the more desirable decisions to make in terms of exercise consequences and may pass the information on to future participants. Informing the new students nullifies the worthwhileness of the simulation as an effective contributor toward enhancing the decision-making capability of students.

The scope of detail incorporated into an exercise is a function of the creativeness and ingenuity of the scenario writers and the objectives to be accomplished. The scenario structures a situation and causes the students involved to perform actions, evaluate among alternatives and to make and test decisions. Scenarios can be made so simply that a group of students may complete the exercise in a few hours. More detailed scenarios may involve students for weeks or months. A critique following the conclusion of a simulated exercise is essential to optimizing the value gained from participating in the exercise.

The scenarios employed at Futura reflect the middle school concept. The simulated exercise must be planned by the staff and students for the support of the student's learning with the middle school concept as a guide; it is not surprising that many scenarios are constructed around the common concerns of students. The common concerns including parents, home, school, peer relationships and self-discovery provide an infinite number of possible exercise situations. After the Futura students become more sophisticated in their decision-making approaches, simulated exercises are undertaken involving topics that can be approached with less emotional undertone. The breadth of exercises undertaken must still be shaped by the requirement th t problems encountered by the players are real and vital to them. The exercises must cut across activities undertaken by the students in the several other discipline areas.

Morrow Town Middle School. Morrow Town's middle school is a mecca in the late 1970's for professionals who want to discover first-hand how students learn to learn. Students at Morrow Town have been discovering how to learn since the mid-seventies. The project resulted from the work of the learning theorists in the late 1960's and early 1970's. The learning theorists discovered many hitherto unknown facts about such learning approaches as inquiry and discovery, reinforcement, assimilation, transfer, insight, frequency, exposition and multisensory involvement. New concepts were revealed concerning storage and retrieval of information in the brain. One of the fallouts of the studies was the realization that individuals differ greatly in their ability to handle learning approaches. Quite often students making little or no progress in a discipline were observed to be using or to being subjected to learning approaches which contributed to the student's difficulty.

The late sixties and early seventies saw industrial concerns, who were interested in obtaining a larger share of the education materials market, devote much effort to the rational organization of material for a given discipline. Discipline experts were employed to compile whatever materials they felt were essential to the mastery of their field. The experts gathered material ranging from very elementary aspects to the most difficult to comprehend. Their work was intended to span the learning period from early childhood through the university. While discipline compilations can never be complete in the sense that the information system becomes closed, many comprehensive compilations were available to the education market place by the mid-1970's.

The professionals at Morrow Town recognized the value of the compilations. The value arose not out of the vast knowledge resources available per se, but rather from the opportunity it afforded to discover how individual students learned a particular discipline. The Morrow Town professionals use the rationally organized materials to discover how children learn. Having ascertained the nature of a student's learning model, the staff can support the student in discovering how he learns and in improving the effectiveness of his learning patterns for the various disciplines. Morrow Town sought the aid of learning theorists to discover learning patterns. Learning theorists were commissioned to construct programs using particular learning theories and combinations of theories to develop programmed learning materials. The materials cover the difficulty spectrum from simple to highly complex. When new students enroll at middle school and are assigned to a teaching team, the professionals responsible for the particular disciplines and the students work very closely with the learning skills specialists in the learning laboratory. Materials are presented to the students through the use of independent study electro/mechanical electrical and electronic devices available as off-the-shelf items in the 1970's. Presentations utilize the programmed learning materials and the appropriate self-study equipment. After experimentation has determined the optimum learning approaches for the learner, the student is again considered for assignment by the middle school. If the student is likely to benefit through the association with a teaching team having members more skilled in the use of learning approaches optimum for the student at hand than his present teaching team possesses, a strong motive for student reassignment is evidenced. After careful consideration of the other factors acting in the situation, a determination concerning assignment is made.

During his years at Morrow Town, the student discovers how he learns. The learning skills laboratory professionals guide the student in an understanding of the niceties of his particular learning approaches and in the understanding of other approaches if and when the student can adapt his behavior to their use. The student will learn how he must evaluate materials to recognize their effectiveness for his learning. Learning becomes fascinating to Morrow Town's students when it is personalized. Morrow Town students spend 40 to 50 percent of their time in independent study activities.

Swift Pace Middle School. One of the anomalities of the 1960's was the swift fleet of time for the adult world and the slow march of the calendar months for the middle schooler. Writers in the sixties wrote tirelessly about the robbery of youth from American children, about the imposition of adult goals and the incessant organization of child activities. While parents rushed feverishly to take students hither and yon, the children endured the activities for the sake of the adults impatiently waiting for childhood to pass. The goal of childhood was to get it over with as soon as possible.

How different the seventies? Let's take a look at the Swift Pace middle school and see a different type of program in action. The program isn't calculated to matriculate all middle schoolers to the University of Oregon or Vanderbilt University. As a matter of fact, it's not college orientated at all; it's student orientated. Think about that for a moment. We said the program is child orientated. Of course, that statement could be made about the Swift Pace middle school in toto.

The goals of Swift Pace middle school center around providing learning support to students to enable them to develop their capabilities to the fullest extent, to instill in students a love of learning that surpasses the selfish bounds of personal interest. Scientists have long been attempting to look over the horizon with scientific equipment. That day of looking over the horizon may be at hand in the years to come. The students of middle school likewise need to look over the horizon at the new world that lies beyond. If the capability to support student learning that transcends the horizon is not here in the seventies, at least the horizon can be pushed back enabling the student to get a wider horizon to horizon view.

Swift Pace middle school features among its activities a program identified as Far Horizons. Far Horizons seeks to have every student in middle school push back the horizon in areas of special interest to him. Determining the area to give special interest to is not an inconsequential task for a middle schooler. Many students select numerous horizon extending areas before dedicating themselves to a given area. It must be made clear that this is not intended to be a covert way of having youngsters choose a profession in the middle school years. It is intended to afford a vehicle for developing inquisitiveness and experimentation, a vehicle for providing excitement and adventure and encouraging originality. Too often schools in the past have not started early enough to point out that rainbow over the hill. When the rainbow is finally sought, the student detects its illusory nature and becomes despondent. Many of you are well aware of the lack of success with rehabilitating school dropouts so that they return to the nation's high schools.

The machinery for bringing a student into the Far Horizon's program is simple but effective. Soon after a new student is assigned to a student team, the teaching team begins to discover the student's interests, his likes and dislikes and his system of values. Having come to know its new student, the team has a brainstorming session with the new student and talks about Far Horizons. If the student indicates interest, the student is invited to attend the Far Horizons large group sessions consisting of instructional and general educational television programs, films, lectures, demonstrations and just plain talk. The television and film presentations are usually scientific or adventure oriented; the lectures are more like talks by people in the community who find excitement in what they are doing and wish to share their excitement with the students of middle school. The demonstrations are supplied by the community industrial enterprises and occasionally by the armed services; the plain talk is by the students who wish to report on Far Horizons projects, to demonstrate constructs they have made, to pass along some exciting news about new discoveries and inventions, and to solicit partners in adventures that they are pursuing. No student is required to attend any of the Far Horizon meetings although news of them are widely publicized throughout middle school.

After the middle schooler has had an opportunity to attend large group sessions, the students interested in Far Horizons are introduced to an "assistant." The assistant is a paraprofessional employed on a part-time basis by the

Swift Pace middle school. To qualify as an "assistant," the person must not only be talented and skilled, but he must have a love for the work that he is engaged in and want to share his work experiences with middle school students. The paraprofessional usually accumulates a small group of five to twelve students. The paraprofessional who can meet informally with his group at the paraprofessional's work station is prized.

Swift Pace has been fortunate in securing its paraprofessionals. For example, the staff has included an artist who worked with his group at the local art museum, a radio engineer who often took his small group to his studios, a science professor who met with his students at the university, a naturalist who conducted field trips through the local parks, a carpenter who took his boys to building sites, and a reporter who took the students through the newspaper composition and printing rooms. Groups meet at middle schools as well as away. Some very desirable paraprofessionals would be lost if the requirement for field meetings was strictly adhered to. Middle school facilities are available both evenings and on Saturday to accommodate the groups.

Professionals and paraprofessionals work closely together to improve the Swift Pace program. The professionals are able to provide student behavior insights that aid the paraprofessionals in achieving closer personal relationships with students while paraprofessionals often can make valuable suggestions for improving material resources in their areas. Swift Pace's implementation of the Far Horizon program made the inclusion of paraprofessionals into the middle school staff mandatory. A beneficial side effect of the program is a growing mutual understanding between the students and the community. Several police officials served in "assistant's" roles. Students come to respect the requirement for efficient police practices while the police officials learn much about factors in the student's life that contribute to resentment and opposition to imposing adult behavior codes on student behavior.

Electronia. Electronics is improving the effectiveness of the school's report to the parent relative to student progress. The old favorite for comparing school system effectiveness—the achievement test—has been relegated to the carriage house preserving the horse drawn carriage for posterity. Where it was formerly possible to confuse an ill-informed public as to a school system's merits because of alleged superior achievement test scores, now such inconclusive evidence isn't worthy of consideration in discussing educational effectiveness. The public of the late seventies denies that the accumulation of isolated bits of information constitutes adequate learning for the emerging space age. Other means have been developed to ascertain student growth. Space age educational interest is in how well students can work independently, how they utilize resources available to learn, how they attack problems, how they arrive at decisions, what directions their inquisitiveness and inquiry are taking them, what their aspirations are, and how well they are communicating with their environment.

Electronia middle school electronics are helping parents to better evaluate the growth rate of their children and the efficiency with which the school is using the resources provided for educational purposes. The activities of all students are recorded on a random basis through the use of cameras, films, magnetic tape and conductive devices coupled to printers. The skills laboratories are equipped with overhead projections and optical systems which make it possible for observers to sit in a monitoring room unobserved by the working students. The monitors can be photographed if desired. It is possible to observe the reaction of the student in real time. Hesitations, uncertainties, inappropriate learning approaches, emotional involvement can be observed as they occur.

Information on each student is obtainable from computer runs—a whole library of material depicting a particular student's activities becomes available for review and evaluation purposes. The parent receives a first-hand account of his child in the learning environment. The teaching team is available to help the parent to interpret and understand what he is seeing, hearing or reading. The type of student progress evaluation that the parents receive at Electronia fortifies the communication link among student-parents-teachers.

Evaluation of the Future Middle School Posture

Predictions made about the middle school in the late 1970's foretell the flowering of the middle school concept. Disallowing a major war or national economic catastrophe, the predictions have a high probability accuracy. Support for the future middle school is gaining momentum on several fronts.

The industrial segment of the economy is looking toward the educational market place. Electronic technology fallout from the defense industry is available for application to equipment and support activities. The lack of adequate learning theories and models of the learning process are detriments to immediate technology exploitation, but by the late 1970's much progress will have been made.

Information is developing at too fast a rate for education to be a fact storing process. Students are faced with the problem of data rates beyond the capability of the human mind to comprehend. Data machinations are becoming the province of automatic devices. The human's task is becoming that of learning how best to approach learning in new areas and to deal with information when it becomes available. This is to say that the student must develop efficient and effective learning techniques, appropriate for himself and the material at hand, and decision analysis capabilities required for decision-making.

Learning is becoming a life-long process. Millions of persons will be adult students in the 1970's. The person who has visions of the changing scene prepares himself to participate in the altered environment. The future is going to make ever increasing demands upon people to seek new horizons. Students who have learned to look toward far horizons should have less difficulty with meeting challenges requiring reorientation several times during their professional careers.

The middle school of the late seventies cannot achieve its developed status without the support of parents and community. Parents in the sixties support change and innovation. The old cliche that richness begets richness is appropo here. The improved learning support provided for students in middle schools will reinforce parental and community willingness for still further changes that lead to still more effective and efficient education for the 10 to 14-year-olds. The support must come in financial as well as moral form. Living standards will continue their upward march. It is estimated that the average national family income will rise to $10,000 per annum by 1975. With increased federal and state support to education along with increased local school revenue, the funds to procure desired resources will become available.

SELECTED READINGS

Evans, Luther H. and George E. Arnstein. *Automation and the Challenge to Education*. National Education Association Project on the Educational Implications of Automation. Washington, D.C.: The Association, 1962.

Mead, Margaret. "The High School of the Future." *California Journal of Secondary Education*, 35:360-369; October, 1960.

index

149